PRAISE FOR *GREAT TEAMS*

"There is nothing more magical than leading a team to great success. Leaders attempt to inspire others and help their teams find success by managing adversity, giving selflessly to others, and finding common purpose. In his latest book on leadership, *Great Teams*, Don Yaeger has done a masterful job of capturing the best in leadership, which will hopefully inspire future leaders."

—MIKE KRZYZEWSKI

Five-time NCAA tournament champion; two-time Olympic-gold-medal-winning basketball coach; head coach of Duke University men's basketball

"I've been an avid sports fan for many years and an advisor to great businesses for nearly as long. When either a team or a business reaches greatness, it does so because leadership has inspired the players or employees to selflessly pursue something bigger than themselves. Don Yaeger does a masterful job of building a game plan for you to use as your team chases excellence. You will enjoy this book."

—JOHN MAXWELL

#1 *New York Times* bestselling author; recipient of the Mother Teresa Prize for Global Peace and Leadership

"Don Yaeger's insight into how great teams are built sure does resonate with me. Among the lessons reflected are my beliefs, too, that winning doesn't depend on *who* you play; it depends on *how* you play. And it isn't practice that makes perfect; it's perfect practice that makes perfect."

—MARV LEVY

Hall of Fame coach, Buffalo Bills

"A great read! Don Yaeger has quantified the systems of championship teams by highlighting the core values that are imperative to all successful programs. This book is the most relevant 'white paper' on the mechanics of competitive greatness."

—SUE ENQUIST

Eleven-time national champion; former UCLA softball coach

"Two things I know are that building a Great Team takes time and it takes a plan. In *Great Teams*, Don Yaeger gives you some of the fundamentals that will help you build the plan that will make your team great. Being part of the amazing list of people he interviewed was a true honor."

—DAYTON MOORE

General manager, Kansas City Royals, World Series champions

"Life is such a dangerous and unpredictable thing. I can't imagine anyone who thinks they can succeed without a strong team around them. The good news is *Great Teams* lays out the simple, clear steps we can all take to build the kind of team that succeeds again and again and again."

—SIMON SINEK

New York Times bestselling author and inspirational speaker

"Truly Great Teams don't come together out of chance. While many have the goal of becoming a Great Team, not many focus on the process. Don Yaeger has studied the process of becoming a Great Team and gets to the core of exactly what it takes. If you want to build a Great Team, you have your starting point in Don's book."

—JAY BILAS

Duke University basketball; ESPN broadcaster

"Everyone wants to be part of a Great Team, an organization achieving big things. As leaders we have to create that place where those who work for us can thrive, can feel valued. In Don Yaeger's book you can discover how the best teams of all time, in both sports and business, achieved those big things."

—HOWARD BEHAR

Retired president, Starbucks International

"We are always looking for authentic leaders who can help evolve our teams' performances to a world-class level with our business results. When you can find someone who has truly studied Great Teams, as Don has here, these lessons are an amazing and impactful resource that every leader should leverage."

—BILL SWALES

North America channel and alliance leader, Oracle

"When Don Yaeger writes a book, you better pay attention. *Great Teams* will be a classic in the sports and business worlds. I couldn't put it down."

"I've spent nearly three decades studying great corporate teams. Don has come at this from the sports angle. What we've both learned is that a handful of well-practiced behaviors separate the middle of the pack from the top. In *Great Teams*, Don reveals those behaviors and shows how you can apply them to your team, whether it is in sports or business. "

"Building a team that is annually competitive is difficult business. It helps to look at those who have done it for guidance. In *Great Teams*, Don Yaeger does that work for you. This books gets two thumbs up."

"I've known Don Yaeger for more than two decades, and I promise there is no one who asks better questions about how to build Great Teams. The lessons he offers here on recruiting, on culture, and on adversity are invaluable if you want your team to become great!"

"For years I have been fascinated by the habits of sustainably successful teams. Don Yaeger's insight in studying those teams provides us all with a strong foundation for our own team success. As leaders we have an opportunity to learn from the best and take lessons from *Great Teams* to heart, because that's what others who win are doing."

"If you work with at least one other person in some capacity, then you are essentially on a team. Don Yaeger has taken the concept of team and broken it down into its most important parts. The fact that he has been able to get an inside look at how championship teams have been built makes this not just a great read but an educational one as well. *Great Teams* truly is a must-read for those looking for new thoughts that can be immediately implemented in the areas of not just teamwork but also leadership."

—KEVIN EASTMAN

Vice president of the Los Angeles Clippers; former assistant coach of the NBA champion Boston Celtics

"I've had the chance to be part of great and historic teams, and there is something special about coming together like that. If you want to have that same experience, my man Don Yaeger is the guy to show you how to make it happen. He spends every day studying the best, so he knows the answers to this question."

—MICHAEL OHER

Super Bowl champion; story featured in *The Blind Side*

"As a business leader, very much like a coach, I want to bring my team every resource I can to help it achieve its full potential. Don Yaeger and his study of Great Teams has been a valuable resource to us, helping us improve our performance! His ability to bring best practices to the business world has served to educate, motivate, and inspire my team!"

—ANTHONY ROBBINS

Vice president, Brocade Federal; 2016 Wash100 inductee

"Don Yaeger has once again crafted a riveting narrative that captures the behaviors and mindsets of champions. This book is a must-read for anyone who wants to understand how they can take their efforts as a leader and teammate to the next level!"

—BERNARD B. BANKS

Associate dean of leadership development and clinical professor of management, Kellogg School of Management, Northwestern University

"Whether my team is in a winning season or losing season, I've got Don Yaeger on the field with me. To have a Great Team, you have to study Great Teams, and this is the champion's playbook."

—RYAN BLAIR

CEO, ViSalus; *New York Times* bestselling author

GREAT TEAMS

GREAT TEAMS

16 THINGS
HIGH-PERFORMING ORGANIZATIONS
DO DIFFERENTLY

DON YAEGER

W Publishing Group

AN IMPRINT OF THOMAS NELSON

Published in Nashville, Tennessee, by W Publishing, an imprint of Thomas Nelson.

Thomas Nelson titles may be purchased in bulk for educational, business, fund-raising, or sales promotional use. For information, please e-mail SpecialMarkets@ ThomasNelson.com.

Any Internet addresses, phone numbers, or company or product information printed in this book are offered as a resource and are not intended in any way to be or to imply an endorsement by Thomas Nelson, nor does Thomas Nelson vouch for the existence, content, or services of these sites, phone numbers, companies, or products beyond the life of this book.

ISBN 978-0-7180-7762-4 (HC)
ISBN 978-0-7180-8057-0 (eBook)
ISBN 978-0-7180-8406-6 (ITPE)

Library of Congress Cataloging-in-Publication Data

Library of Congress Control Number: 2016933596

Printed in the United States of America

19 20   LSCH   10 9 8

To Jeanette, Will, and Maddie:
Thanks for being my Great Team.
I love you more than any book can express.
DY

CONTENTS

Contents

INTRODUCTION

What Makes a Team Great?

There is something special about watching a Great Team at work. Whether it is on the gridiron, on the diamond, on the hardwood, or in a corporate setting, when a group of people "click," the environment feels electric and the outcome is often extraordinary.

In Major League Baseball, the St. Louis Cardinals and the Chicago Cubs use the same bats and balls and are in the same division—only 316 miles separate their home stadiums—but the historical outcomes for these two iconic franchises couldn't be any more different. Over the last century, the Cardinals have won eleven World Series championships and nineteen National League pennants—the most by any team in the league. By contrast, the Cubs have zero World Series titles and haven't won a pennant since 1945.

What enables the Cardinals to do what the Cubs cannot?

The answer: a hyperfocus on team culture.

The Cardinals know how to win, and they build Great Teams around that knowledge. They develop a network of homegrown talent that doesn't suffer when talented players leave or retire, so they are able to replicate greatness season after season. Thanks to a devoted fan base, the Cubs are financially successful, but the Cardinals win both on the books *and* on the diamond. They have success in every aspect of their operation, from the clubhouse to the gift shop to the boardrooms, as well as within the St. Louis community. Love them or hate them, the Cardinals are a testament to the power of a Great Team and an extraordinary team culture.

Are you looking to replicate such a culture in your own team? The sports world has many parallels to business. Among the strongest of those links is that the teams—and companies—that "win" sustainably spend time building the team culture that allows them to do so. In my previous book, *Greatness: The 16 Characteristics of True Champions*,[1] I examined the various ways an individual can pursue greatness in his or her own life. A few years later, while speaking on this topic to a team at Microsoft, I was presented with a new way of thinking about greatness that took these ideas to the next level. "I appreciate the stories you share about how individuals work to become great," Microsoft executive Eric Martorano said to me after one of several presentations he hired me to do with his team. "But what makes a Great *Team* great?"[2]

This question inspired me. The pursuit of individual greatness is a great first step, but what happens next? What does greatness look like when it moves from the personal space to a team context? Why are some teams inherently more dynamic, effective, and healthy than others—even if their collective resumes look identical in terms of ability, drive, and experience? More important, why can some teams remain competitively relevant for long periods of time while others fluctuate in effectiveness and results?

Before I could begin to study Great (and not-so-great) Teams in the sports and business worlds to look for patterns and consistencies, I first had to establish the standard for greatness that I would be using to evaluate each group. Is greatness more than winning championships or reaching sales quotas? Can a team reach its goals and not be "great"? What makes a group of people come together in a way that doesn't just work, but really produces chemistry? What sets a truly Great Team apart from one that gets the job done, but in a cloud of conflict or even just a fog of mediocrity?

I set out to find the answers, traveling the world to talk to the greatest team builders for instruction.

During scores of interviews with the list of Great Team builders you'll find in the appendix, it became apparent that these teams are driven to create a culture of greatness. Trendy offenses, tricky defenses, or "hot products" often get the credit for success, but the truly amazing organizations don't stay at the top of their marketplaces without building a team-first culture.

Now, *culture* is a buzzword that is all over the business publications these days, so I think it's important to define it. In considering how the word specifically applies to a team setting, I came up with two possible definitions: 1) the conditions within the organization that promote either growth or failure and 2) the shared understanding of what to do in adverse situations.

The effort to achieve that culture can be broken down to four essential pillars that I believe set a truly Great Team apart from one that simply performs well:

- **T**argeting Purpose—The team is connected to a greater purpose. Members understand whom they are serving and why that matters.
- **E**ffective Management—The team is able to think creatively and act dynamically in order to stay fresh, effective, and relevant.
- **A**ctivating Efficiency—Each member of the team brings a unique set of talents, experiences, perspectives, work ethic, personality traits, and know-how that melds with and complements those of the other team members.
- **M**utual Direction—There is a strong sense of understanding, appreciation, shared responsibility, and trust that unites and motivates the team to work together.

After studying the subject carefully and discussing it with these truly great leaders, I found sixteen defining characteristics that special teams— the ones that are in a class by themselves, that accomplish more than just a winning season or a successful fiscal year, that pack extra punch and bring a degree of excitement to what they do—all share. These traits can be worked on independently by individual team members, but the truly outstanding teams use them to build on one another. Organizations that exhibit real greatness combine talent, relationships, and innovation in a variety of ways for the sake of achieving a shared goal.

In the following pages you will encounter a wide variety of examples

Pillar One

TARGETING
PURPOSE

CHAPTER 1

GREAT TEAMS UNDERSTAND THEIR "WHY"

They are connected to a greater purpose.

Every day, whether it's at practice or a game, an important meeting or an ordinary day at the office, the highest-performing teams show up with a sense of purpose; they understand the "why" of what they do and can clearly see how it matters. The better an organization understands whom it serves, the more effective it will be in weathering challenges along the way.

For this reason, a Great Team will constantly remind its players and employees that they are involved in something larger than themselves and their individual goals. Some team members will instinctively grasp this essential concept and will appreciate and respect the tradition of what they do or whom they work for. Others will need reminding, and leadership must intentionally create emotional moments that connect them to their greater purpose. But whatever the case, understanding the deeper motivation behind the effort is one of the most important elements of a truly Great Team.

GREAT TEAMS IN SPORTS

In the early years of the twenty-first century, reconnecting with the true purpose of playing for their country became the driver that allowed members of the US men's basketball team to return that program to elite status from the brink of disaster.

The 1992 Olympic tournament in Barcelona, Spain, had been an unmitigated triumph for Team USA, who won its games by an average of 43.8 points on the way to a gold medal. This had been the first year professional athletes were allowed to play in the Olympics, and the US "Dream Team" had been determined to show the world that when its best players were on the court, they simply could not be beaten.

But in the following years that sense of purpose waned, sputtered, and eventually lost steam. By the 2000 Olympics in Sydney, Australia, international teams had cut Team USA's margin of victory in half. In fact, one game came down to a critical two-point win over Lithuania—thirty points closer than the narrowest game played by the Dream Team in 1992.

"The awe factor was gone, and the players from other countries were now either playing in US colleges or in the NBA against our players," said Jim Tooley, CEO for USA Basketball, the nonprofit organization that runs the team. "More significantly, international teams had some-thing we didn't have—continuity. Their teams were together many, many years in a row. It was a big deal in many of these countries to be on your national team, and the best players always wanted to be on the team together. On Team USA, we were shuffling new players in every year."

There were other problems, too, all connected with a loss of purpose. Team USA spent very little time educating its players on the significance and honor of playing in the Olympics. It also spent little time or energy scouting opponents, Tooley said. As a result, by 2002, international competition had caught up. Team USA went 6–3 in the FIBA world cham-pionships and finished sixth—a mere decade after the Dream Team. In the 2004 Olympics in Athens, Greece, the team was a failure both on and off the court and ultimately took home the bronze medal. The poor result wasn't because the team lacked talent. In fact, the team was built around five players who are or will be first-ballot Hall of Famers.

USA Basketball had clearly lost its "dream," and the losses prompted some much-needed soul-searching within the organization. "We just picked guys in 2002 and 2004 and said, 'You have thirteen days to train—let's go,'" Tooley said. "In comparison, you had international teams who had been together for a long time, knew the intricacies and etiquette of the game, and understood the responsibilities that came along with being an ambassador for the game and your country."

There were valuable lessons to be learned in the difficult losses, however. The organization realized that what had worked in the early 1990s no longer applied and that the team needed to reengage with its central purpose. Tooley described this time as rough from a professional standpoint, but possibly "the best thing that could have happened to us."

In 2005, the Olympic program brought in Jerry Colangelo to be the managing director of USA Basketball. One of his immediate changes was to reinforce the team's connection to its patriotic purpose and to minimize the attention that had been devoted to the individual players. Colangelo understood that the focus needed to be on the *program* and what it represented, not the recognized superstars. So one of his first changes was to have the size of the players' names reduced on the jerseys and the USA lettering enlarged.

"When you put a uniform on with 'USA,' you're diminishing the player's name," Colangelo said. "I wanted our players to regain respect for what it meant to represent their country."

Colangelo also changed the committee format of selecting players and sought to have more consistency in the coaching staff—hiring a permanent coach instead of changing leadership every four years. He wanted to promote and sustain a single vision over a period of time, and he argued that without continuity and consistency, players would not buy in to the long-term goals of the team.

When it came time to choose a new coach, Colangelo selected Mike Krzyzewski of the Duke University Blue Devils to lead the team. Krzyzewski agreed with his new boss that Team USA's problem wasn't one of talent but of *culture*. The players had stopped appreciating the importance of what they were doing and why it mattered that they show up every day prepared to play like champions.

Krzyzewski—a West Point graduate and US Army veteran—suggested that the team needed "feel-it moments" to drive home that players were now involved in something greater than themselves and to fortify the foundation of the team.

"You can try to tell people why what they do matters. You can try to show them. But people get what it means when they can feel it," Krzyzewski said. "Our job is to make sure that our teams always feel what it is we're playing for."

Krzyzewski's feel-it moments were meant to galvanize the team around more than just winning. To bolster this new sense of purpose, USA Basketball formed a partnership with the US military so the players could feel what it meant to represent their country in a different way.

"We want to stress patriotism and a passion for selfless service in our team," Krzyzewski said. "Who better to share that example than members of the armed forces? They live those commitments every day, and I wanted our guys to see, hear, and feel what that meant."

Using the military connection, Mike Krzyzewski repeatedly sought out ways for Team USA to understand its greater purpose. On the way to the 2006 world championships in Japan, for example, Team USA detoured to Korea. In between team practices, the players wore fatigues and dined and lived with soldiers protecting the Demilitarized Zone. This immersive experience strengthened the perspectives of the players by helping them understand the responsibilities, disciplines, and daily sacrifices of defending American freedoms.

As the Beijing Olympics neared, it had been eight full years since the United States men's basketball team had taken home a gold medal in the Olympic Games. But recruitment for the 2008 games proved not to be a problem. The very best American players—Kobe Bryant, LeBron James, Dwight Howard, Dwyane Wade, Chris Paul—were actually lining up to play for new leaders Colangelo and Krzyzewski, all because they wanted to be a part of the team's revitalized and purposeful culture.

The players took representing their country seriously, and their commitment showed in Beijing. Team USA went 8–0 on the way to a gold medal, winning by an average of twenty-eight points a game. In the championship game, Team USA defeated international powerhouse Spain by eleven points. The win created waves of basketball fever across the United States. Around the world, international fans and sports media alike began to love Team USA again.

Winning that gold medal was more than a victory for Team USA. It was also an important example to our nation and to the world that the organization represented more than just basketball; it was also a symbol of national culture, honor, and tradition. After the victory, even more NBA players took notice, and Team USA was flooded with potential recruits who desired to play for the team and take their patriotic responsibility seriously.

In the years that followed, USA Basketball maintained the connection to its "why" by continuing to partner with the military, creating more and more "feel-it" moments for the players. For instance, just before the team left the country for the 2012 Olympics in London, Krzyzewski took his players to visit Arlington National Cemetery. They made their way to Section 60, where many of the most recent casualties are buried, and saw a soldier paying his respects to his fallen comrades. Krzyzewski asked the man to speak with the team, and everyone gathered around to listen to his spontaneous, moving words. When he finished and departed, Krzyzewski turned to his players and said, "That's why we came here—to feel our country."

It was the very definition of a feel-it moment, and it deeply affected members of Team USA—especially forward Kevin Durant of the Oklahoma City Thunder, who admits to being forever changed by the visit to Arlington National Cemetery.

"It was overwhelming," he explained. "You really get a sense of what our soldiers are doing for us every day. I just want to play harder, just sacrifice. That's all. I may not shoot as many times as I do in Oklahoma City, but this is my small sacrifice, and I know that is important. It is really fun to do that because you know you're doing it for a greater purpose that's bigger than you, your family, and where you come from."

Team USA's players internalized the experience, and their strengthened sense of why they were playing made a big difference at the 2012 Olympic Games. The results were incredible: Team USA was even more dominant than in 2008, winning by an average of thirty-two points per game on its way to gold, including a record-breaking eighty-three-point victory over Nigeria.

MORE FROM THE GREAT TEAMS IN SPORTS

Great Teams in sports remind their players on a daily basis of the significance of their history: the important things the team has done and for whom they have been done.

The St. Louis Cardinals—winners of the 2006 and 2011 World Series—have utilized this lesson and condensed it into the principled lifestyle and harmonious playing style they call the Cardinal Way. The phrase has become a catchall term to describe every facet of the Cardinals organization, which has been built on high professional standards. Bill DeWitt, managing partner and chairman of the Cardinals, says that this code of conduct ensures a "continuity of success."

"The Cardinal Way is excellence throughout all aspects of an organization," said DeWitt. "It's making sure that everyone from top to bottom is on the same page, and our goals and objectives continue to be at the forefront of Major League Baseball." This includes engaging new recruits in a culture of high character and developing players by stressing fundamentals of play and sportsmanship.

DeWitt credits the Cardinal Way philosophy with providing organizational stability because of the club's traditional roots. "Each decade since the 1920s, our organization has had championship teams or Hall of Fame players that have added so much to our program," said DeWitt. "We feel a great responsibility to continue that culture of excellence."

By appreciating team history and applying it to current demands, the Cardinals have been immensely successful at integrating their "why" into the organization's professional philosophy. The results show on the field. The Cardinals have won eleven World Series titles and have made the playoffs eleven out of the past fifteen years.

Kevin Eastman, who has coached for both the Boston Celtics and the Los Angeles Clippers and currently is vice president of basketball operations for the Clippers, has unique knowledge of what it's like to build a winning culture—he's done it with a team that has a great tradition as well as one with a lackluster tradition. With the Celtics, it was important to draw on the legacy of greatness evident in the seventeen championship banners hanging from the rafters of the team practice facility in Waltham, Massachusetts (a duplicate set hangs in Boston's TD Garden, where the Celtics play their home games). Eastman and the coaching staff would regularly bring in Celtic legends such as Tommy Heinsohn and John Havlicek to speak with current players. The goal was to never let the team forget what it meant to be a Celtic or what expectations come with being in the organization.

"Culture must be reminded every day," Eastman said. "The history gives us a starting point to learn from the past, produce in the present, and prepare for the future."

But what if you're leading a team or organization like the Clippers, who lack such a storied tradition? Eastman says that team leadership has to emphasize to its players that they have the opportunity to do something new, to establish that winning culture and create "a legend for future generations."

"Bad history or no history—frame it," said Eastman. "Frame it to your advantage. If you have a great record of success, stress it. If you don't, tell your team that they get to go out and make it. Whatever it is, use your history to create energy for your team."

AND FOR THE TRULY GREAT
TEAMS IN BUSINESS

In the business world, a "why" is often misunderstood as a company mission statement or code of ethics—which couldn't be further from the truth. Author and inspirational speaker Simon Sinek has described a company's corporate "why" as "always disconnected from the product, service, or the act you're performing."

If an organization desires to become a Great Team in the business world, then it must understand how to utilize the "why" properly in order to galvanize support from its professional ranks. "When an organization lays out its cause, how it does so matters," explained Sinek. "It's not an argument to be made, but a context to be provided. An organization's 'why' literally has to come first—before anything else."

The Declaration of Independence is a primary example of this distinction. It provides a thorough context of belief at the very beginning: "We hold these truths to be self-evident, that all men are created equal, that they are endowed by their Creator with certain unalienable Rights, that among these are Life, Liberty and the pursuit of Happiness."[1]

The declaration would have read much differently if it had begun with a list of grievances against the king of England. Instead, it starts with the *belief*—or deeper purpose—as to why the colonies felt justification for creating a new country. The beliefs and desires of our country's founders are stated precisely but not without emotion in this document. It stands as the epitome of a "why"—and a Great Team's context of belief—that changed the world.

Companies that understand the purpose and philosophy behind the "why" are usually astute, high-performing organizations that tap directly into the pulse of those they benefit the most. When utilized correctly, this understanding can create a powerful sense of duty and purpose for business teams because the employees know exactly whom they are working for and to what end.

Great companies connect to the heartstrings of their employees to make their purposes known. Bill George, former CEO of Medtronic, the world's largest medical technology company, considers the emotional connection between Medtronic employees and the organizational mission to be "one of the greatest achievements" of the company. Though Medtronic consistently leads the medical industry with its innovative therapies and products (a fact stock analysts love), George considers the company's annual holiday party to be the true highlight of the company's year.

During this special event, all the employees at the company's operational headquarters in Fridley, Minnesota, assemble in the company's auditorium—along with thousands of other colleagues watching via webcast—to hear from families of patients who have received Medtronic products. These families recount the ways that Medtronic devices have bettered their lives. After they are finished, there is never a dry eye in the room. "Every year, it seems, a young woman steps up and says, 'Thank you. Because you did your job so well my father got to walk me down the aisle this summer,'" George said. "That never gets old."

Through the personal stories and feelings of the patients, the Medtronic employees are able to reconnect annually with just how important their work is. It's not about just making money for themselves or the company, but making a difference in the lives of others. By seeing the impact of what they do on real men, women, and children, the employees are able to understand the great, life-changing scope of the company "why."

George said this dynamic is even more important as workforces are getting younger. "There is lots of research that says millennials are driven to work for companies they believe are engaged in doing good," George said. "And as more of our workforce comes from that generation, we have to make sure they know what we're doing and can appreciate its importance."

The late Steve Jobs, cofounder, chairman, and former CEO of Apple, was heralded for the landmark vision of his computer company, Apple. Apple's particular brand of personal computing revolutionized the technology world and went on to sell millions worldwide, but that was not

Jobs's "why." His greater vision behind Apple was to empower people and to make the personal computer easy enough that everyone could use it.

This deeper purpose can be directly observed in much of Apple's advertising and Jobs's speeches during his tenure at Apple—especially the Orwellian-themed 1984 commercial that promoted the Apple Macintosh computer as an amazing tool that would give people the power to rise up and make demands from society. Jobs and Apple sold America—and ultimately, the world—on the belief that one individual could actually compete against an entire industry by using an Apple product. That belief was Apple's "why."

Southwest Airlines considers excellent customer service an important part of its culture. CEO Gary Kelly even gives a weekly "shout-out" to employees who have given outstanding performances. Southwest also does profiles of standout employees in its in-flight publication, *Southwest: The Magazine* (formerly *Spirit*) as well as circulating videos within the company that share stories of exceptional service. Southwest reinforces its culture, just as the Boston Celtics do, by talking about it all the time and celebrating those who are working today to keep that history alive.

A company that is highly philanthropic can help employees feel the greater importance of their work by strengthening the connection with their community. Advisors Excel, an insurance marketing organization, is an excellent example of a company that uses this strategy. In 2014, employees helped build and outfit a home for a single mother of four in their home city of Topeka, Kansas. The company also turns its annual employee and customer conference into a fundraiser for charities such as the V Foundation for Cancer Research, the Make-A-Wish Foundation, and the USO. The philanthropic "why" is strong at Advisors Excel, and its employees are regularly reminded that the company not only wants to be profitable but also cares about making a difference in the community and the world. Doing good in the community is so important to Advisors Excel that the company regularly highlights and praises its employees for their efforts, thereby reinforcing the importance of the stated corporate values.

Modern science, incidentally, supports the idea that a philanthropic orientation can be highly advantageous to a company. Michael F. Steger, associate professor of applied social and health psychology and counseling psychology at Colorado State University, developed the Work and Meaning Inventory (WAMI) for businesses. Steger's tool processes "meaningfulness" according to the degree that employees find their work to have significance and purpose, the contribution their work makes to their finding broader meaning in life, and the desire and means for their work to make a positive contribution to the greater good.

Researchers have also found a link between meaningful work and job satisfaction. According to the Gallup State of the American Workplace report for 2010–12, the vast majority of employees are not engaged in their work, and this disengagement currently costs US companies 450 to 550 billion dollars in decreased productivity a year.[2] Providing employees with a culture that emphasizes charity and purpose is an exceptional way for them to feel the meaningfulness of what they are doing and give them a sense of job satisfaction beyond simply hitting sales figures, client counts, or other basic metrics of performance.

If you were to ask most CEOs what their organizations' number-one priorities are, they would probably give predictable responses about company growth or increasing stock value. But when would they mention their own people? Unfortunately, it is very common in the business world for employees to be far down the list of priorities. The Great Teams in business, however, emphatically support their people. Without happy, engaged employees, a company won't have organizational growth or the dependable workforce behind increasing stock value.

"The order matters," said Sinek. "It reveals whether you have a sense of purpose or not."

While most companies tout the importance of corporate culture and have made it a talking point, few have actually made a priority of shaping that culture around a shared purpose. Instead of a "why" to motivate and unite team members, these companies have only a set of performance goals and targets—not enough to motivate a team to greatness.

"Leaders have to set the tone at the top for the vision of the company and have to walk with a purpose," said Bill McDermott, CEO of the multinational corporation SAP SE. (The *SAP* name stands for Systems, Applications & Products in Data Processing, and the *SE* is roughly the European equivalent of *Inc.*) "It's the things that you repeatedly do when things get really hard that tell the world who you really are."

McDermott's company, the global market leader in enterprise software, specializes in creating custom programs for specific problems and has more than 291,000 customers in 190 countries. But despite SAP's immense size and reach, it clearly understands its "why"—the fundamental connection to the role it plays in the lives of its customers and how that role directly affects the economy.

"In our case, we really felt that helping the world run better and improving people's lives was our enduring mission," said McDermott. "Furthermore, businesses that care a lot about improving people's lives with [their] solutions are far more likely to not only make a difference in the world, but to also be relevant in the twenty-first-century economy."

A prime example of this is the Walt Disney Company, who uses SAP technology to manage its theme parks—which in turn allows hundreds of thousands of starry-eyed young children to create lifelong memories with their parents. McDermott said that this is "authentically" what SAP does and that people's lives run better because of it. This is what makes his company's "why" so great.

"All we have to do is recognize the things that we do in service to companies ultimately impact the lives and enjoyment of consumers," said McDermott. "If we can stretch our mind to start there, we can create great companies."

GREAT TAKEAWAYS

Having the most talented team does not guarantee success. The talent must also be unified around a culture that makes the overall purpose for the organization clear. The buy-in from employees comes from having more than a theoretical understanding of their working importance; the real connection between employee and employer comes from actually feeling and experiencing that importance in their daily operations. As Coach Krzyzewski said, it is important that every team member *feel* what the team values together.

Perhaps the "why" can be revealed through purposefully focusing—or refocusing—the shared purpose, as happened with the St. Louis Cardinals and Team USA. Maybe, like the Boston Celtics and Southwest Airlines, an organization can look to the past for inspiration in discovering its "why." Odds are that veteran employees who have been through the highs and lows of a company's history have experiences and wisdom to share, and their past battles and victories can help the current team understand how to achieve future success. Perhaps, as SAP demonstrated, a company can begin by understanding its customer's "why" and using that to spark motivation for consistently high performance. Or maybe a team can follow the example of Advisors Excel by recognizing excellence and identifying good examples of employees who have a clear understanding of the team goal. This can be leveraged into framing the way leaders and team members interact as they celebrate those who do great things.

If a good team desires to become a Great Team, it must consistently communicate its "why." Everyone must be aware of a purpose that is greater than producing revenue. Profitability matters, of course, but the bottom line should never be the biggest "why."

When buy-in does occur, leaders and managers must not miss the opportunity to show the good results that come from a company's work, create "feel-it moments" that evoke serious passion, and find unique ways to put the team's overall goal into perspective. A shared experience can energize a team toward its common goal more quickly than a direct order ever will.

May your team discover your "why."

Pillar Two

x
 o

EFFECTIVE MANAGEMENT

CHAPTER 2

GREAT TEAMS HAVE AND DEVELOP GREAT LEADERS

They sustain success by placing a high value on leadership.

There is no question that the key to any organization is leadership. From the CEO to frontline staff, strong leaders are critical to performance. It is no coincidence that every issue of the *Harvard Business Review* features an article or case study on this quality. In professional sports, the saying is that a team is only as good as its owner. And while every team and business has a leader, many organizations lack a culture of leadership development within the ranks. Great Teams that sustain success place a high value on developing leadership. Promoting such a culture leads to consistent behaviors and better habits and ultimately increases that team's chances of winning.

Brad Black and his organization, HUMANeX Ventures, provide laser-accurate leadership surveys for some of the most successful teams in sports and business. CEO Black considers professional assessments a "foundation of development" and essential for any leader desiring to be great.

"Context matters," Black said. "If you were told that you were the Olympian of your chosen profession, then you'd have a context [on which] to base your strengths. And all leaders should have a strong sense of who they are before they attempt any developmental venture."

Black is right. All leaders should know where they—and their teams—stand on skills, strengths, weaknesses, and latent talents. Black said that understanding who you are as a leader is a "gift to yourself" and can create the road map for your own growth.

From this chapter, you'll learn the five most common leadership styles, along with the principles for developing an effective system of leadership that fits your team.

COMMAND AND CONTROL

Bobby Knight. George Patton. Martha Stewart. Al Dunlap. These are all well-known leaders who have employed what I call Command and Control governance. This approach is autocratic in nature and does not involve their subordinates or followers in the decision-making process. They prefer to tell versus lead, and they are highly concerned with the details of what their teams do. Typically, these individuals micromanage aspects of their teams' strategies.

Command and Control leadership usually conjures up a negative stereotype, but it can be enormously successful. Just look at the track records of those mentioned above. Such individuals ensure that an organization's long-term vision remains intact. This can bring order to a disorganized company or clarity during a crisis.

Additionally, competent Command and Control leaders excel at reinforcing strong team cultures. Consider the Pittsburgh Steelers, who have won six Super Bowls—currently more than any other team—largely because of the Rooney family. The Rooneys have owned the team from its inception in 1933, and either father Dan or son Art can be found in the Steelers front office on a daily basis. The Rooneys have built and maintained a team with remarkably consistent leadership through all levels of its organization.

Amazingly enough, the team has had only three head coaches—Chuck Noll, Bill Cowher, and Mike Tomlin—over the past forty-five years. Though leadership turnover is low, a revolving roster of players creates a unique challenge for Steelers management in reinforcing important aspects of team culture such as humility, hard work, and accountability of self and community—what Coach Tomlin has described as "the careful management of everything you do, every day." The Rooneys' insistence that those in leadership roles embrace the daily challenge of implementing this culture is one reason the Steelers have proved to be so consistently successful.

"Continuity is something that you can benefit from, but it is not something you can take for granted," said Coach Tomlin. "I want everybody in the building to know what it is we are doing and what our focus is. What is acceptable, what is unacceptable—and cultivating an environment that fuels that for me."

RELATIONAL

For Relational leaders, people come first. These managers strive to keep their teams happy and in harmony. They are approachable and employ a "come with me" style of leadership.

A Relational leader can be very good at building trust, respect, and employee buy-in as a result of letting people have a say in the decisions of the company. In the business world, CEOs Sarah Blakely of Spanx and Tony Hsieh of Zappos head wildly successful companies, but both are known for their even-keeled leadership and for engaging others in decision making.

Joe Torre, who now serves Major League Baseball as executive vice president for baseball operations, spent much of his career managing MLB teams such as the New York Yankees. As a manager, he was quick at recognizing the contributions of individual players and did not miss an opportunity to express his gratitude to them. He elicited trust from his players, which in turn encouraged his team to play harder for him. Torre created a Relational environment that allowed him to get the most out of some very talented athletes who were not as successful when playing for other organizations.

Sometimes the individual members of a team have to be led differently, according to their personalities or learning styles. Anson Dorrance, head coach of the University of North Carolina women's soccer team, knows this very well. In 1979, Dorrance, who had begun his career as the head coach for UNC men's soccer, expanded his role to developing the women's team for the university. He quickly discovered that there are big differences between coaching men and women.

"Part of being a leader is getting to know your players," said Dorrance. "I learned that with men it was often a matter of just telling them what needed to be done and then showing them how it was to happen. Coaching women, from my experience, required a different touch. What you're after when you are coaching young women is seeing where they are extraordinarily special and unique. Once you know that, it becomes your conduit to leading them. I know those are very general statements, but it reminded me how I needed to look at everyone I was asked to lead and see them differently."

Through Relational leadership, Dorrance established one of the most successful records in athletics. Under his leadership, the Lady Tar Heels won twenty-one NCAA women's soccer championships. This legacy is due in part to Dorrance's understanding the value of properly relating to his players.

EXPERT

Great Teams are often led by visionary leaders who are sponges for information and knowledge and who depend on their high levels of knowledge or specialized sets of skills to guide their teams. These are the Expert leaders. Experienced in nearly every aspect of their professional spaces, they have immense clout; those in their presence are motivated to listen because their expertise is so vast.

In the corporate world, Bill Gates was an absolute Expert as the chairman, CEO, and chief software architect of Microsoft Corporation. From

1976, when the company was founded, through 2014, when he left as the company's chairman, Gates charted Microsoft's product strategy by aggressively broadening its product range. Microsoft Windows, his most famous multipurpose operating system, was a worldwide sensation and made the company a household name. And though Gates's leadership style was known to have ruffled a few feathers, it is ultimately responsible for making Microsoft the dominant tech giant it is today.

Likewise, no one questioned the authority of Phil Jackson when he was head coach of the Chicago Bulls and Los Angeles Lakers. His knowledge of the game—from recruiting to the *Xs* and *Os* of play calling—was second to none. Jackson was able to coach some of the greatest basketball players who ever lived—Michael Jordan, Scottie Pippen, Kobe Bryant, and Shaquille O'Neal. He not only brought out their absolute best but also stimulated buy-in for his vision from these highly competitive athletes. This showed on the court time and time again. Jackson's Expert philosophy and approach to basketball produced eleven NBA championship titles.

CHARISMATIC

Imagine a leader with a personality so engaging and inspiring that you hang on his or her every word. These are people who don't tell you what to do but create a vision of what you can do and light the fire to make you want to rush out and accomplish it all. Charismatic leaders tend to be incredibly skilled at reading an environment, scanning and processing the moods and concerns of both individuals and larger audiences, and honing their actions and words to suit any situation. This connective strength enhances the trust employees have for their leaders, creating even greater success. And while the skills are often innate to the personalities of the leaders, they can also be practiced and honed to improve any organization.

President John F. Kennedy possessed this kind of charisma. An exceptional communicator, he gave the world some of the most memorable speeches of all time. Every time he spoke with the press or to the public, he had a mission to convey not only a feeling but an undeniable truth. Kennedy's charisma and authentic passion could be felt in every single word, which was why he was so good at connecting with the hearts of his audiences.

Pete Carroll, head coach for the Seattle Seahawks and former head coach for the University of Southern California Trojans, is known across the sports world for his cool-headed temperament and engaging personality. Throughout his career he has managed to handle intense scrutiny and pressure, overcome setbacks, and maintain an optimistic perspective on life and football—all while being highly successful. Carroll's charisma has allowed him to perform at a championship level in the entertainment mecca of Los Angeles as well as in Seattle, a city of discerning taste.

Charismatic leadership, like Command and Control leadership, can have its downside, especially if practiced by a selfish or short-sighted individual. At its worst, it can be manipulative or divisive or lead to eventual disillusionment. But when practiced responsibly, charismatic leadership can bring an organization to life—boosting recruitment, inspiring loyalty, and building trust—all vital components in building and maintaining Great Teams.

Trust, especially, can be a crucial element. For nearly three decades, the Great Place to Work Institute has studied the greatest workplaces around the world, with annual data representing more than ten million employees in fifty countries. Business leaders, academics, and media analysts have all relied on the metrics from Great Place to Work to establish strong cultures and build high-performing work environments. The institute's research consistently reveals that trust is the single most important characteristic in making a workplace great. And building trust can be a strength of a Charismatic leader—if that leader takes steps to maintain that trust as well.

China Gorman, the former CEO of Great Place to Work, examined some of the most successful leaders in business and determined that they all create value-based cultures that are dependent on faith and trust. "In all decisions, leaders must always conscientiously ask themselves, 'Will this build trust with my employees or is it going to tear trust down?'" said Gorman. "It doesn't matter whether you are in health care, the aviation industry, financial services, or a large tech company—it still applies. The great workplaces have a foundation of trust."

Recruiting and cultivating talent is another key team-building element in which Charismatic leaders shine. Gorman strengthened the organizational leadership in her own company by building a culture that allowed her team to "attract the right talent" and support that talent. "A great culture allows its talent to do its best work and choose to come back every single day in order to exceed the expectations of all stakeholders," said Gorman. "It is just an incredible virtuous circle" (a positive cycle of events in which one good thing leads to another). "And it all begins with leadership behavior."

SYNERGISTIC

Command and Control leaders and Expert leaders tend to hyperfocus on details, which they may prioritize over developing their subordinates into leaders, and both of these leaders tend to lose crucial time over-analyzing. In contrast, Relational leaders can face diminishing returns by spending too much time connecting with their teams. Charismatic leaders run the risk of being perceived by their teams as self-absorbed or disingenuous.

Synergistic leaders, on the other hand, balance the best characteristics of the other four styles, so they have the best chance of establishing a Great Teams culture. These leaders have visions for their teams, but also the ability to empower others to be innovative; they advance the needle of progress though all aspects of their teams, easily adapt to change, and develop others in their ranks. Some may argue that Synergistic leaders can be prone to inconsistency, largely because they draw from so many wells of leadership. But if they keep their focus, these leaders can take teams to great heights.

John Wooden, the legendary head coach of men's basketball at the University of California, Los Angeles, was the epitome of a Synergistic leader. He was not only the greatest men's college basketball coach of all time, but was arguably the best in sports history. In the sports world it is difficult to make statements like that without debate, but I do so confidently in light of Coach Wooden's immaculate character, his principled leadership, and his inarguable success on the court. During a twelve-year period of his twenty-seven-year tenure at UCLA, the Bruins won the NCAA championship ten times—with a record eighty-eight-game winning streak and four undefeated seasons. Coach Wooden accomplished these feats while constantly shuffling his roster to account for graduating seniors and incoming freshmen. His leadership proved to be the foundation of a seamless transition.

For Coach Wooden, building team culture involved a process, and he used elements from the other leadership styles to establish a culture based on integrity and accountability.

He demonstrated a solid Command and Control approach, for instance, by enforcing standards among his team, especially in making sure his players knew they were at UCLA first and foremost to get an education. Ultimately his leadership established a strong educational pedigree for many UCLA superstars—such as Kareem Abdul-Jabbar, Bill Walton, and Marques Johnson—all of whom graduated before heading to the NBA. Other players went on to have highly successful nonathletic careers after their collegiate basketball careers were finished.

Coach Wooden's rules for his teams were simple and consistent: never be late, never use profanity, and never criticize a teammate. He also developed the Pyramid of Success, a visual showing fifteen "building blocks for a better life." Coach Wooden defined success as "peace of mind, which is a direct result of self-satisfaction in knowing you made the effort to become the best that you are capable of becoming."[1]

But Coach Wooden veered from the Command and Control

management style in that he didn't just give orders and expect them to be followed. He led by being a living example to his players—even down to the way he dressed. For games he always wore a suit and tie, and his hair was meticulously well-groomed. He also made a personal resolution never to lose his cool on the sidelines; he believed that if he lost his composure, his players might do the same thing. He was able to ingrain his leadership into his players by living his ideals every single day; if he said it, he meant it.

Wooden exhibited Relational leadership by getting to know his players and tailoring his coaching to suit their individual talents, weaknesses, and learning styles. "Some coaches tear people down, but Wooden built confidence in everybody," said NCAA and NBA legend Bill Walton. "He knew how to make 12 people complement each other all the time. Coach Wooden would always tell us not to play to the level of our competition, but to play as though we were playing against the ideal performance. . . . That was the beauty of John Wooden. He was always pushing us every day, but never talked about winning."[2]

This Relational aspect of Coach Wooden's leadership extended to his staff as well. He expressed it this way in an interview late in his life: "Another very important part of leadership is to make those under your supervision feel that you care for them—not just for the job they are doing for you."[3]

Coach Wooden believed that selling the vision of what could be accomplished by the organization was a valuable component to great leadership. Charismatically, this is where he shined; Wooden emphasized praise on and off the court by acknowledging bench players during press conferences and requiring his players to credit teammates after every basket. He believed in providing empathy and compassion for the people he led. And to reach his players on a very subtle yet powerful level, Coach Wooden coined inspiring leadership phrases that were easy to remember and apply, such as, "If you don't have time to do it right, when will you have time to do it over?"[4] Other favorites of his were, "Be quick, but don't hurry,"[5] as well as, "Winning takes talent; to repeat takes character,"[6] and, "You have not taught until they have learned."[7]

Coach Wooden was more than just a fountain of positive affirmations, however. He was a student of the game and had converted his extensive knowledge into Expert leadership. He knew that successful leaders studied others in their fields, and he made a habit of doing so every off-season, regardless of his team's success.

Coach Wooden was especially adept at the art of adapting his coaching plan to his ever-changing team roster. He believed that failing to adapt the game plan to the players would lead to failure. So he began each season with a change in philosophy on how to win. His focus would be geared specifically to that season's team.

In 1964, for instance, UCLA had no player taller than six-foot-seven. At the suggestion of assistant coach Jerry Norman, Wooden implemented the full-court zone press defense to compensate for his players' lack of height. The winning principle that year was simple—to emphasize the ability of UCLA's smaller, quicker athletes rather than trying to play conventionally. The strategic move worked, and UCLA went undefeated that season. And in the national championship game, when UCLA faced Duke and their two six-foot-ten players, the overall athleticism of UCLA still won out, and they captured their first title.

Coach Wooden's unorthodox thinking, along with understanding his roster well enough to be competitive, was essential to making UCLA a champion that season—and solidifying him as an Expert leader. And he didn't stop there; Wooden deftly leveraged this strategy into a recruitment tool and selling point for future players across the country.

Through Coach Wooden's Synergistic leadership, three decades of college basketball players were inspired to achieve success both athletically and professionally. His ability to inspire and direct others toward excellence has been widely recognized as a major force behind UCLA's college basketball dynasty—and is an outstanding example for any leader to follow.

GREAT TAKEAWAYS

To lead effectively, you must have a sense of what kind of leader you are.

Are you a Command and Control type who micromanages your organization?

An Expert who draws from a wide variety of experience?

A Relational leader who consistently seeks to build up your team?

A Charismatic one who charms them into buying your vision?

Ideally, I think, we'd all like to be leaders who are Synergistic in nature, who incorporate the best of the other leadership types. And the good news is that we can be. Although most leaders tend toward one style or the other because of their basic personalities or backgrounds, leadership style is not set in stone. Every leader is capable of learning and adapting in order to build a Great Team.

In particular, great leaders must consider not just their own leadership styles but the styles their teams *need* in order to be very successful. Any team can perform to standards with adequate leadership. But for a team to shatter expectations and become great, the leader must set the tone. Leaders must understand the importance of whom they are leading but also know which approaches work best to create competitive advantages—and be able to adapt their own tendencies to provide what is needed.

Regardless of style, every leader must understand and be willing to implement certain leadership basics. First, they must establish cultures that hold all team members accountable for the outcome of collaborative efforts while also allowing them to participate by providing ideas. Second, they must make sure that there is consistency between their expectations for others and their own actions.

At the simplest, most practical level, this means that a leader who demands that employees be on time must set the tone by being on time as well. If employees are expected to put in extra time at critical moments, the leader must work overtime too. Leaders who take these basics to heart will be in a better position to develop their teams for ultimate success.

Great Teams

With that in mind, I invite you to take advantage of the exercises at the end of this chapter, which are designed to help you determine your current leadership style.

And keep in mind that while good leadership often leaves well enough alone, great leadership *adjusts*.

EXERCISE: Assessing Your Leadership Style

Instructions: For each pair of the personal preferences listed below, place an *X* in the box that most closely matches your preference. For example, if you strongly prefer coaching a player to participating yourself, place an *X* in the 1 column. If you strongly prefer playing a sport to coaching it, place the *X* in the 4 column. Place the *X* in the 2 or 3 column if you are somewhat in between. Rate each pair the same way. Next, count the number of *X*s in each column and multiply that number by the value of column. For example, if there are 3 *X*s in the 2 column, multiply 3 x 2 and get a 6. Add the resulting numbers to determine your Decisiveness Factor.

Follow the same process in the next exercise to find your Empathy Factor. Then plot your numbers in the corresponding pages to identify your quadrant. The result will be your base personality style.

WHICH IS MOST LIKE YOU OR DO YOU AGREE WITH THE MOST?

	1	2	3	4	
I want to coach someone on how to win at a game					I want to play in the game
I want to help the team					I want to lead the team
I'll ask everyone in the group where they want to eat lunch					I'll just pick a place and ask everyone to meet me there
I like to think long and hard about decisions					I like to make quick decisions

Great Teams

	1	2	3	4	
I'm okay when people are a few minutes late for meetings					I believe meetings should start and end on time
I prefer people who give and take					I prefer people who pick a position and stick with it
"Better to be safe than sorry"					"Always push things right to the edge"
"Take your time"					"Let's roll!"
I believe it's okay to be average at a few things					I believe I should always shoot for greatness, no matter what the task
I prefer quiet reflection					I prefer to talk things out
I prefer reading a book					I prefer trying a new outdoor sport
I prefer to lead people by showing them what to do					I prefer to lead people by asking them to figure it out
I prefer comedy movies					I prefer thrillers
I think it's best to hold your tongue when working in a team					I think it's best to let people know what you think when working in a team
TOTAL Xs					
Multiply by column number					
Total Decisiveness Factor					

EXERCISE: Assessing Your Leadership Style

Instructions: To determine your Empathy Factor, evaluate yourself on this second set of personal preferences. Use the same rating process and mathematical formula you just exercised to find your Decisiveness Factor.

WHICH IS MOST LIKE YOU OR DO YOU AGREE WITH THE MOST?

	1	2	3	4	
I like to stick to a schedule					I like to wing it
I like math					I like art
I would rather be a doctor					I would rather be an actor
I think problems are best solved by following the directions					I think problems are best solved by finding others who can help
I think problems are best solved by gathering a lot of information before taking action					I think problems are best solved by trial and error
I keep my worries to myself					I tell my worries to whomever will listen
People come to me when they need serious answers					People come to me when they need a laugh
I hang back in a large crowd					I meet as many new people as possible in large crowds

Great Teams

	1	2	3	4	
I like formal restaurants					I like casual delis
I prefer people who are reserved					I prefer people who like attention
I drive right around the speed limit					I drive ten miles over the speed limit
I like people who fit in					I like people others consider weird
I search the web for days when making a big decision					I feel like too much information makes my head spin
I prefer small gatherings					More is better when getting together with friends
TOTAL Xs					
Multiply by column number					
Total Empathy Factor					

EXERCISE: Assessing Your Leadership Style

Instructions: Mark your two totals on the graph below. For your first factor, Decisiveness, draw a vertical line where your number lies on the axis that runs left to right. For your second factor, Empathy, draw a horizontal line where your number lies on the axis that runs bottom to top. Then plot the point where your hand-drawn lines intersect.

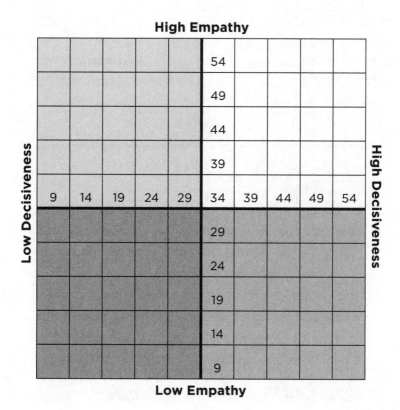

EXERCISE: Assessing Your Leadership Style

Instructions: Transfer the point where your hand-drawn lines met on the previous graph to this one. That point will identify your likely leadership style.

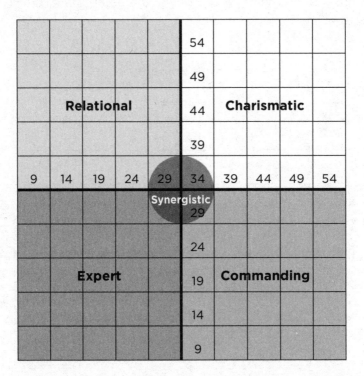

For more free exercises that guide you in using your leadership style to your team's advantage, visit teams.donyaeger.com.

CHAPTER 3

GREAT TEAMS ALLOW CULTURE TO SHAPE RECRUITING

They realize that fit is more important than credentials.

Purpose and leadership are essential to building a team culture. Once an organization determines its "why" and aligns its leadership style with the needs of its members, it is on the right path to becoming a Great Team. But culture building doesn't stop there. A team must also recruit the right talent. If done well, recruiting will result in a highly competitive team that is consistently motivated to seek and claim success.

Great Teams recruit players who fit—who will thrive within the established team culture and add value to it. The talent of the employee or teammate is important, but fit trumps all. These organizations understand that Great Team culture establishes an environment conducive to success, but that success ultimately depends on the right kind of personnel.

Ray Conner, CEO and president of Boeing Commercial Airplanes, shared with me that creating a positive culture is personal in every way. "With culture, you have to create it in a way that people can connect, and they can see themselves as a contribution," Conner said. It "has to be set up . . . so everybody can say, 'Yes, this is what we are about and that is what we want to be.'"

In today's marketplace, it is very easy to be wowed by decorated resumes. When the "ideal" candidate—the one with the outstanding CV—arrives, many leaders incorrectly believe that including that person will automatically better the team. A Great Team, however, understands that fit is more important than credentials. Someone who might be perfect for one environment—or might have been great while working for a competitor—will not be a guaranteed fit for another.

How can you recruit to find the best fit for your team? In this chapter you will learn how to identify the best prospects for your team culture and how to ensure that new team members are shaped by the culture you've spent so much time establishing.

FINDING A-CALIBER RECRUITS

Kevin Ryan, an online entrepreneur and founder of Business Insider and online-shopping juggernaut Gilt Groupe, once said, "The best use of a CEO's time is to bring in unbelievable people, manage them well, and make sure the company builds and maintains an A-caliber team."[1] Ryan is certainly correct. But in order to assemble an A-caliber team, you must recruit A-caliber players—people who are on the rise, who have high potential but not necessarily extensive experience, and who show promise to achieve superior performance early in their tenure with your organization. These players exhibit behaviors that are in line with the organizational culture and the values of the team. They typically desire to be part of something bigger than themselves and have a magnetic attraction to a strong company "why." Ultimately, A-caliber players refuse to settle for anything less than their best, which is exactly why leaders must be skilled at finding them.

Recruiters often have difficulty spotting an A-caliber player because they are distracted by impressive resumes, dazzled by the current accomplishments or the educational background of "superstar" candidates. Unfortunately, leaders who evaluate candidates from a limited perspective often make critical mistakes—such as viewing high performance in an employee's current or past job as a guarantee for future high performance in a new role.

NBA Hall of Famer Isiah Thomas won two NBA championship titles as point guard with the Detroit Pistons, but as head coach of the Indiana

Pacers and the New York Knicks, he had only a .456 winning percentage in five NBA seasons (187–223). Thomas performed even more poorly when coaching for Florida International University (26–65) before leaving the program in 2012.

Similarly, consider hockey great Wayne "The Great One" Gretzky, holder of sixty National Hockey League records and 894 career goals scored. But as hot as he was on the ice, he turned cold when he made the move to coaching. His Phoenix Coyotes never made the playoffs in four NHL seasons, accumulating only 143 wins and 161 losses before Gretzky stepped down.

Thomas's and Gretzky's coaching careers show that it can be counterproductive to hire based on credentials alone—no matter how good the candidate looks on paper. As leaders, we must shop the market for A-caliber employees who are suitable for our teams' cultures and likely to be comfortable in our corporate environments.

But what if you are considering hiring the best player on a rival's team? In 1989, the historic Herschel Walker trade between the Dallas Cowboys and the Minnesota Vikings rocked the sports media world. Many questioned the intelligence of the Cowboys organization for dealing away not only their best player but one of the best running backs in the league—for several draft picks.

But the Cowboys leaders, who were rebuilding under first-year head coach Jimmy Johnson, saw an opportunity that the general public didn't. "Once a season is over, a weight of expectations are realized," said Johnson. "Team leadership has to learn from previous streaks and reinvent themselves. What you did last year won't work this year."

Johnson figured the best way to rebuild his roster with winning players was to trade leading rusher Walker to Minnesota for a treasure trove of future potential. The Vikings, who felt they were on the verge of having a championship team, could not resist the deal. The previous year, Minnesota had finished with an 11–5 record and made it to the second round of the NFL playoffs. Vikings management was convinced that Walker would be the final piece to propel the team to a Super Bowl title.

However, Walker's league-leading talent didn't translate. His running style didn't fit with the offense the Vikings had already built, particularly its blocking scheme in the running game. In essence, the Vikings had picked the wrong employee to handle a crucial job.

While Minnesota managed a 10–6 season after the trade, it lost in the first round of the playoffs. In 1990 the Vikings fell to 6–10. By 1992 Walker was no longer with the team, and the Vikings had made wholesale management and coaching changes.

In contrast, Dallas parlayed the draft picks it had received from the Walker trade to acquire several A-caliber players—including Emmitt Smith and Darren Woodson. This strategy ultimately led the Cowboys to three Super Bowl titles in a four-year span.

MORE FROM THE GREAT TEAMS IN SPORTS

The world of sports has its share of mediocre recruiting examples, but there are many other examples of organizations that have seen value in a recruit's knowledge, skills, and attitude and ended up with an ideal fit. When connected with a productive team dynamic, this kind of recruitment is a recipe for greatness.

Chris Petersen, current head football coach of the University of Washington football team and former head coach of the Boise State Broncos, is a master at making these connections. While at Boise, he built a powerhouse by recruiting players other schools were not pursuing. Under his leadership, the Broncos amassed an incredible record of ninety-two wins and thirteen losses, five bowl wins, and two undefeated seasons. Petersen made Boise State relevant by recruiting what he called "OKGs," or "our kind of guys."

"There was a tremendous price to pay in order to play on [Boise's] blue turf," said Petersen. "You couldn't be the normal college student. We needed that special, humble player who is going to sacrifice and make their life simple."

Petersen's ideal OKG is a person with character, a great attitude, a willingness to make an effort, and—most important—toughness and football IQ. These qualities matter far more than size or a flashy highlight reel.

"In the business of recruiting, everybody falls in love with the tape," said Petersen. "But you must remember to fall in love with the *kid*, not the tape. We really tried to hone in on the OKGs because [not] all of the really good guys . . . get the same attention."

In a 2012 *Sporting News* poll, Petersen was ranked as the second best coach in college football, with only Nick Saban of the University of Alabama Crimson Tide besting him.[2] The two head coaches and programs couldn't have been more different. Between 2009 and 2012, Saban recruited eighty-five of the top high-school players in the nation, while Petersen signed only *one* four-star recruit. But during that period of time, Petersen defeated some of the best teams in the nation— including Alabama and the University of Oklahoma Sooners—with OKG players who had never even appeared on the recruiting radar of the larger programs.

Petersen looked at several specific areas to determine if recruits fit the mold of a Boise OKG. "We just try to do as much history as we can, talk to the kid and the people who surround him," he said. "We want to tell the recruit what we are all about and find out what they are all about. I tell them that our place is much harder than other places and our standards and expectations are different than a lot of programs."

He also paid close attention to the core GPA of a potential player, because he believed that score "painted a picture of that recruit" and indicated whether a recruit would fit with the university's emphasis on the intelligent athlete. Petersen—who was the self-appointed academic liaison for his team—held players accountable to the Broncos' culture and enforced academic excellence. He expected only the best efforts from his players, both on and off the field. "You must know that you are a student here first, and [you] have to be willing to sacrifice in order to make the team better."

"Leadership gets what it emphasizes," Petersen stressed. "When the recruits arrive to campus, there's so much hype in the facilities and the winning. But we tell them that all of the hype will not be their happiness. Instead, their happiness will be in the coaches we surround them with and how we treat them in the locker room. Culture will determine their happiness."

Petersen's honesty about the Boise program and culture gave recruits a clear idea of what to expect—a great example of an organization truly understanding the power of the right fit.

Common recruiting logic typically examines the top 25 percent of the team and then attempts to replicate the characteristics perceived to belong to the talent in that top quarter. The challenge of that strategy is confirmation bias—leaders have no way of knowing those good qualities aren't also present in the bottom 75 percent as well. A Great Team digs deeper until it finds differentiators that set its recruits apart from the rest of the field. "And when that happens," Peterson said, "we've done something right."

Great recruiting of A-caliber talent can create championship teams, but only if the players who are recruited match the existing culture or help it grow in the desired direction.

It is important to recognize that vastly different team cultures can create champions as long as they recruit the right fit.

Over the span of the 1989–90 and 1990–91 NCAA men's basketball seasons, the University of Nevada, Las Vegas Runnin' Rebels and the Duke Blue Devils built one of the most intense rivalries in the history of the sport. The beauty of that rivalry is that it extended to nearly every facet of how those teams were built and even to what the schools represented, especially in terms of the players who were recruited.

The UNLV team projected a gritty toughness, and that was not by mere coincidence. Hall of Fame coach Jerry "Tark the Shark" Tarkanian felt he needed players who were true rebels, who could handle the bright lights of Las Vegas and feel comfortable playing in a city with so many distractions. Tarkanian often looked for tough-minded inner-city kids from one-parent households. He wanted to bring in hard-edged survivors to become college basketball's toughest and meanest squad. His recruits included Larry Johnson, Stacey Augmon, Anderson Hunt, and Moses Scurry, all of whom came from hardscrabble backgrounds.

The 1989–90 NCAA championship game between the Runnin' Rebels and the Blue Devils showcased UNLV's gritty mentality and revealed their true brand of tough-as-nails basketball. The Rebels capped off their finest season with a thirty-point blowout victory over Duke, dunking and taunting their way to the title. They were widely criticized for their showboating, but Tarkanian's understanding of his environment and team culture helped them become champions.

The Blue Devils, meanwhile, had also developed a reputation congruent with the team's environment. Duke University was viewed as an upper-crust, Ivy-League-caliber school that was looking to improve its national reputation in the realm of athletics. The private school used basketball as a way to generate more interest from top students around the country and thus improve the pool of talented student-athletes it could recruit. But that meant Duke had to recruit a certain type of player who could fit into the social fabric of the university as well as head coach Mike Krzyzewski's more disciplined style of play.

"We look for talent and the academic potential to stay enrolled and not become overwhelmed," said Krzyzewski. "The third thing is, most importantly, character—what kind of kid is he? For us, it's not about one- or two-parent households because kids can be from anywhere. But are they good guys? How are they in class?"

The "good guys" he recruited tended to pick up the team culture quicker because they had already been exposed to Duke-style values by their current teams or families. "These guys all come from families where they listen to their parents, coaches, and teammates," Coach K said. "We also evaluate how they react when their coach talks to them in a huddle and how they celebrate their teammates."

Krzyzewski's faith in the elite Duke culture set the bar for the team. Additionally, it allowed him to ensure that culture thrived by recruiting athletes who fit the image that the university was trying to develop—players like Grant Hill, Bobby Hurley, and Brian Davis. Despite changes in the landscape of college basketball, with more players forgoing graduation to sign professional contracts in the NBA, until recently Krzyzewski's players regularly stayed all four years in college and graduated.

Thanks to the Rebels' victory over Duke the previous year, the rivalry was heightened, and the 1991 Final Four matchup between UNLV and Duke gave Krzyzewski's Blue Devils the opportunity to embrace this new battle of cultures. The Rebels were undefeated (34–0) going into the game and played to their "bad boy" label, but the Duke "good guys" were prepared. From the opening tipoff, Duke showcased an extremely disciplined style of play. Power forward Christian Laettner scored twenty-eight points, and freshman Grant Hill chipped in with eleven key points, helping Duke upset UNLV 79–77 before moving on to win the national championship.

Duke and UNLV used two completely different strategies while recruiting, but they both knew how to find players that fit their cultures. And by doing so, both teams became champions.

AND FOR THE TRULY GREAT TEAMS IN BUSINESS

According to the *Harvard Business Review*, A-caliber players are four times as productive as average employees—a universal truth seen across industries. Tech-giant Apple reports that A-level developers are nine times more productive than the average programmer. Top sales representatives deliver eight times more revenue than the average rep. In the operating room, high-performing transplant surgeons have a success rate six times higher than the average transplant surgeon.[3] These individuals don't settle for less but consistently pursue greatness—and an organization cannot be successful without them.

But how do you distinguish A-caliber players from the rest of the talented field of recruits? The answer: look for unique qualifiers that correspond to your team culture. CEO Tony Hsieh of Zappos, whose Relational style of leadership was profiled in the previous chapter, uses "weirdness" as a unique differentiator to determine his A-caliber recruits. Hsieh asks potential employees to rate how "weird" they are on a scale of 1 to 10 and usually picks those who rate themselves near the top of that scale. While unorthodox, his strategy is actually appropriate because the Zappos culture isn't based on conservatism. So for Hsieh, his A-caliber players are people who see themselves as regularly moving outside of their comfort zones and being able to contribute strange, new ideas to the organization.

"Our philosophy at Zappos is that we're willing to make short-term sacrifices . . . if we believe that the long-term benefits are worth it," wrote Hsieh in an op-ed for the *Harvard Business Review*. "Protecting the company culture and sticking to core values is a long-term benefit."[4]

Clearly, the short-term sacrifice has paid off. Hsieh has used the "weirdness" of his team to transform Zappos from a modest online company into a worldwide sensation with more than a billion dollars in revenue per year. And it all began with knowing what recruits would fit well into the preexisting company culture. A candidate might have unbelievable credentials and expert-level skills, but at Zappos, if you are self-conscious of putting yourself "out there," then you just don't fit.

Target, America's second-largest retailer, with annual revenue of $73.7 billion, keeps ahead of the highly competitive retail market by deliberately recruiting employees who value diversity and thrive on overcoming challenges. The organization views the uniqueness of each employee as its greatest strength; this appreciation of uniqueness is a reflection of how its team views the world and approaches work. Two key components of the Target culture are inclusion and celebration, which together create an environment where everyone feels valued and uplifted. As an extension of that culture, Target's Technology Services program and its Hispanic Business Council regularly provide community outreach programs and training in order to close diversity gaps. Through these efforts, the organization has effectively filled its ranks with A-caliber players who understand the importance of diversity and how it will ultimately shape the world of tomorrow.[5]

Attracting A-caliber talent may require an organizational culture to adapt to the times. According to the US Bureau of Labor Statistics, more than eighty-three million millennials were born between 1982 and 2000[6] and will one day take leadership roles vacated by Baby Boomers and Generation X. Millennials, as a group, tend to have a strong desire for an empowering work environment, and some of the largest, most innovative companies in America—such as Google, Apple, and Facebook—have taken notice. These companies use qualitative and quantitative data to help drive accurate recruiting.

According to data collected by the Intelligence Group, 64 percent of surveyed millennials desire to make the world a better place, 79 percent want a boss who will be a mentor, 88 percent value collaboration over competition in a work culture, and 88 percent seek "work-life integration."[7] This is an indicator for why so many millennials are flocking toward Silicon Valley, where many companies have adjusted their corporate cultures to match what the up-and-coming workforce truly wants in a career.

GREAT TAKEAWAYS

Sports teams and business organizations base their recruiting on what they can offer new team players and what the players can offer in return. There is no sense in signing someone who doesn't suit your playing style or whose goals don't match those of the team, franchise, or organization. Prospective recruits may be supremely talented, but if they don't fit within the culture of the organization, their talents may never have a chance to flourish.

The Great Teams—such as the Boise State Broncos, the UNLV Runnin' Rebels, the Duke Blue Devils, Zappos, and Target—have mastered recruiting to their cultures, and any organization seeking similar success must look within before blindly searching for the perfect candidate. Leaders should assess their team dynamics, search for any limitations, and evaluate the possibilities of the culture. By identifying the drivers of success or improvement within the organization, a team can be well on its way to creating a great recruiting strategy.

Stephen Covey, the well-known author of the *The 7 Habits of Highly Effective People*, once wrote, "If you can hire people whose passion intersects with the job, they won't require any supervision at all. They will manage themselves better than anyone could ever manage them. Their fire comes from within, not from without. Their motivation is internal, not external."[8]

The passion that Covey mentioned can be easy to discover for keen organizations that truly understand fit. Leaders who evaluate the knowledge, skills, and attitudes of candidates in light of their teams' existing dynamics can quickly determine which recruits are right for their companies and which are not. This process can make all the difference between a candidate's success or failure and can save an organization time that would have been spent on trial and error with the wrong candidate. As Bob Reinheimer, former executive director at Duke Corporate Education, said, "The right recruiting strategy brings in people who, over time, strengthen and build to the culture. But the wrong employee does more damage and inevitably creates more friction."

An organization must ask new team members to embrace the established team culture and concepts, which include the team's past and future. That means the organization's leaders must make a point to understand the concepts and culture in order to articulate why a recruit should want to join their team. Such reflections can provide deep insight for any organization seeking to obtain A-caliber members.

As for the recruits themselves, they should desire to be part of the team, its culture, and its vision; they must believe in something greater than themselves. When a team recruits new members who are in line with the goals, practices, and philosophies that define the organization's culture, the attraction—and ensuing relationship—will be powerful.

CHAPTER 4

GREAT TEAMS CREATE AND MAINTAIN DEPTH

They build a deep bench at all levels of the organization.

O nce the leaders of a Great Team recruit A-caliber players who fit the culture, they continue the process by building depth in the organization. Depth provides suitable replacements for key players and a sense of calm in moments that can be perceived as tumultuous by members of the team.

The top-performing sports and business organizations all operate on the principles that 1) no team player is irreplaceable and 2) talent must be shaped in order to build a deep bench at all levels of the organization. One of the best ways for leaders to do this is to create healthy internal competition. The right kind of competition within an organization can bring out the best performance and growth of A-caliber recruits and high-potential employees.

Additionally, Great Team cultures develop strategies for improving the quality of depth at various positions within the organization. Implementing intense practices or creating a learning environment can enhance both the skill level of individual players or employees and the depth of the team positions.

In this chapter you will learn how to identify your high-potential team members (your "high potentials") and keep them engaged, as well as how to develop healthy competition within your ranks.

GREAT TEAMS IN SPORTS

The Los Angeles Lakers franchise has a storied history, filled with example after example of organizational depth. Over the last half-century, the depth of the Lakers roster was a major factor in the team's domination. That depth—and the internal competition it drove—was the reason the team's history includes twenty-one Hall of Famers and sixteen NBA championship titles. The franchise employed a formula for success by building and adding depth around high performers.

However, the Lakers' organizational success began to crumble in 2011, when front-office management decided to build the franchise around a single player—NBA all-star Kobe Bryant. Though Bryant is tremendously talented, his struggles with injuries directly affected the Lakers' performance. In 2013 Bryant tore his Achilles tendon, and the Lakers were swept in the first round of the NBA playoffs. The very next year, while Bryant rehabbed from a knee fracture, the Lakers were the third worst team in the league. The team showed only minimal improvement in 2015, while Bryant nursed an injured shoulder. That year the Lakers were the fourth-worst team in the NBA.

Despite this history of injuries, Bryant remained the highest-paid player in the NBA for several years running. The Lakers organization made the conscious decision to focus all of its energy and resources on this one superstar, and in so doing the management limited its salary-cap options. This organizational failure prevented the team from creating depth around Bryant, surrounding him with adequate talent. The Lakers paid a heavy cost for navigating away from a principle that once made the franchise so special—a cost that intensified when Bryant retired at the end of the 2015–16 season.

Jerry West, the Laker legend whose silhouette is the one used in the NBA logo, said that building depth is "crucially important" to long-term success.

"If you don't have someone on your team that's a capable replacement, then you're going to have a hole in the picture of your puzzle," said West, who would go on to be the team's general manager for many years after his playing days were over. "If a player leaves and there is no replacement, then the team is not complete. Soon everybody will get frustrated because they can't find that missing piece. And I think that's the key to it. A team needs to have enough depth among its good players just in case something goes wrong."

West, currently a senior advisor of basketball operations for the 2015 NBA championship–winning Golden State Warriors, said that great coaches understand their best players won't be in the game every day—mentally, physically, or emotionally—and they know the value of strategic substitutions from their depth charts. West used these lessons in helping to build the Golden State Warriors, who had the best record in the NBA in 2015.

"One of the most difficult tasks is finding players who are willing to accept who they are and that they are not going to be a starter," said West. "Those are invaluable to a team."

The concept that one person's presence or absence can make or break a team is antithetical to how a team should operate. An organization that lacks depth places immense responsibility on the shoulders of a few.

This can be a crucial mistake, as the Indianapolis Colts learned during their 2011–2012 season. When their superstar quarterback, Peyton Manning, sustained a neck injury and missed the entire season, the team suffered. They won only two games that season because they did not have a backup plan in the event of Manning's absence.

By contrast, when St. Louis Rams quarterback Trent Green was injured in 1999, backup quarterback Kurt Warner took over. This deep-bench substitution led to the Rams' first Super Bowl win and sparked a three-season run that is famously known as the "Greatest Show on Turf."

In 2001, little-known Tom Brady stepped in for injured Pro Bowl quarterback Drew Bledsoe and proceeded to lead the New England Patriots to a Super Bowl victory. Brady was promoted to starting quarterback and over the next four years led the Patriots to two more league championships.

And before Warner or Brady ever threw a football, a deep bench played a vital role in the greatest NFL season of all time. The 1972 Miami Dolphins boast the only undefeated season in NFL history, and the achievement is even more impressive because of a critical injury the team was able to overcome early in the championship campaign.

During the fifth game of the regular season, star quarterback and future Hall of Famer Bob Griese suffered a broken leg and ankle—an injury that usually dooms a team's chances of achieving any level of success. But Miami was prepared. Prior to the season, Dolphins head coach Don Shula had made the decision to bring in thirty-eight-year-old veteran backup quarterback Earl Morrall. Shula had acquired Morrall in April 1972 for the price of only one hundred dollars, but the two had history; they had first met in 1960, when Shula was the defensive coordinator for the Detroit Lions. Later, when Shula became head coach of the Baltimore Colts, he had brought Morrall with him to back up the legendary Johnny Unitas.

Morrall was extraordinarily experienced at leading Great Teams. He had already made two Super Bowl appearances and started nearly every game during the 1968 season, when the Colts played the New York Jets for the title. Shula's strategy of bringing him to the Dolphins meant they had a proven player who was willing to play a backup role even though he had the desire and skill set for a starting role.

Before the 1972 season, Shula had described Morrall as "an intelligent quarterback" who wasn't going to be overwhelmed by the moment. Shula was right. While many teams would have faltered in the face of adversity, Morrall's competitive drive and approach to preparation prevented any major lapse in productivity.

Quarterback wasn't the only position with a deep bench in the Dolphins organization. Coach Shula also recruited an assortment of talented running backs in Larry Csonka, Jim Kiick, and Eugene "Mercury" Morris. Shula created this depth in the running back position as a backup plan for the wear and tear of his starting quarterbacks. The more Shula's running backs had the ball, he reasoned, the less fatigued his star quarterbacks would be.

It was an ingenious strategy—with an additional benefit. Each player fed off the knowledge that the other could easily replace him and perform just as well, if not better—and this internal competition provided the perfect driver for improvement. Together they dominated opponents all season long, with Csonka and Morris both rushing for more than a thousand yards and each averaging more than five yards whenever they touched the football.

After Griese's leg injury, Morrall started the remaining nine games of the regular season and opened the postseason as starting quarterback. Morrall led Miami to a first-round playoff victory against the Cleveland Browns but was pulled in the second-round playoff game against the Pittsburgh Steelers because Griese was healthy again.

Rather than fight Shula's decision to play Griese, Morrall accepted the demotion. "I can't say I liked it, but I wasn't going to create a problem," Morrall said years later. "We were trying to win a championship, not worry about people's feelings."

When Griese returned to the game, he was particularly sharp and focused, leading his team to a win over Pittsburgh and then over the Washington Redskins in Super Bowl VII—the culmination of a perfect, undefeated season for the Dolphins.

Shula's emphasis on having such depth on the 1972 team is one of the underlying factors of its success. The play from both quarterbacks and all three running backs over the regular season and postseason generated the type of competition all Great Teams should aspire to have. Essentially, Shula created a culture of not just backup players and backup roles, but also backup plans. As a leader, he was famous for playing out one what-if scenario after another with his coaches and players to challenge them to consider alternatives. This is the kind of contingency plan any team or organization should be ready to execute in case its personnel changes.

The Miami Dolphins went on to win a second Super Bowl victory in 1973, proving that proper depth at vital positions was the key factor in Miami's untouchable spot in the NFL history books.

MORE FROM THE GREAT TEAMS IN SPORTS

The UNC women's soccer program, run by head coach Anson Dorrance, is a perfect example of the role internal competition plays in creating depth. With an astounding twenty-one NCAA championships and 625 victories, Dorrance has mastered the ability to create depth with his high-potential players—and it all begins in the practice facility. Dorrance refers to his practices as the "competitive cauldron" where he and his staff measure every drill, scrimmage, and exercise and then rank players according to what they observe. This public performance evaluation encourages improvement from lower-ranked players while motivating the top performers to work hard to remain at the top.

"What I love about the competitive cauldron is the immediate feedback and also what it projected back into the practice," said Dorrance. "That increases engagement, concentration, focus, and also competitive fire."

The competitive cauldron is a powerful motivator for generating healthy competition within the team. "The three most critical elements in athletic character are self-discipline, competitive fire, and self-belief," said Dorrance. "If you can impact one-third of that on a consistent basis with record keeping and then make a public posting, then the player gets to decide if he or she likes being on the bottom or is motivated not to ever be there again."

Creating depth on a team is not immediate. Sometimes it takes team leaders years to effectively build a deep bench and then shape their recruits through competition. This defies the expectation of instant gratification that is so prevalent in our society.

When Dayton Moore joined the Kansas City Royals as general manager in 2006, he asked fans to remain patient as he restructured the ball club. And taking the time to reorganize proved to be a wise investment. As fans waited during the losing seasons that followed, Moore was building the future of the Royals through his farm and recruitment system. That future would include back-to-back winning seasons and a World Series title in 2015—the club's first in thirty years.

During that long buildup, Moore was driven by a very simple philosophy: care for everyone in the organization as if he or she were family. "Our secret is caring more for our players," he told me in an interview. "We may not outsmart or outwork other teams, but what we can do differently for our players is care more than anybody else. They want to know that you are going to do everything that you can to help them succeed and that you really care about what they are experiencing."

This leadership criterion was applied to Moore's executive team and coaching staff as well. All new hires were asked hard questions about their willingness to follow the program the Royals had laid out to develop talent from within, even if it meant suffering some losses in the meantime.

Moore and his scouting team evaluated potential players on moral principles with a unique qualifier—positive relationships with their fathers or other male role models. They found that these individuals were more likely to respect authority, show discipline, and thrive on competition—all ideal fits for the Royals organization.

"The mission was very simple: let's create an organization that we'd want our own family to be a part of," said Moore. "Even when interviewing staff or evaluating talent, we'd ask ourselves, 'Do we trust these individuals to be around our family? Can they improve through competition?' Character is always revealed, and we wanted people working for us who could show those moral principles each and every day."

"It is your job as a leader," he added, "to make sure that you are all doing your part to help create the best working environment that you can while remaining vulnerable, transparent, and learning from your mistakes."

It took Moore seven losing seasons to reshape the team for long-term success. In that time, he created one of the best farm systems in Major League Baseball—the secret to the team's impressive depth.

The Great Teams know that success is the culmination of persistent communication, consistent performance, and pursuit of long-term goals—through winning seasons or losing ones. A good team can ultimately become a Great Team if it develops talent and leadership at the right pace.

AND FOR THE TRULY GREAT TEAMS IN BUSINESS

Just as a good coach has a plan to replace a starting player, a business leader must have a plan to replace a key employee. This is one of the most helpful and necessary parts of creating depth in a company. Even when it's not feasible to hire from outside to fill a vacancy, it makes sense to plan for a replacement from within the organization and prepare that person for the new responsibilities.

Renter's Warehouse CEO Brenton Hayden used this principle to prepare for the departure of one of his most valuable employees—himself. Hayden founded Renter's Warehouse with the idea of leaving the business after several years to pursue other ventures. With this plan in place, he crafted his corporate structure so that he developed functional depth at the top of the organization first.

Foremost on his list was the creation of a succession plan. Hayden identified the employees within his organization who were his key backups and then exposed them to all areas of the business. He was transparent about his plan and encouraged these individuals to take additional responsibility in the business. The ownership that Hayden encouraged in his workplace allowed for a seamless transition to a new CEO. Likewise, the depth he created prepared the organization to survive and thrive after he left.

Hayden's situation is, of course, an unusual one, in that his company had plenty of time to prepare for his departure. That's rarely the case—another argument for building depth into an organization. Corporations, like sports teams, need to be prepared for the worst. When a key team member is lost early into a project or receives an offer elsewhere, the remaining members of the company must have confidence in the replacement.

The unexpected nature of business can make this difficult, however, especially when an organization is battling high turnover—and high turnover seems to be the wave of the future. According to a 2013 study by the Hay Group, organizations across the globe are in a worldwide trend of accelerated turnover. Over the next five years, average employee turnover rates were expected to rise from 20.6 to 23.4 percent, and by 2018, 192 million workers were predicted to walk away from their companies.[1] These rates include high potentials, the employees an organization needs most to develop depth.

Obviously, high turnover works against the development of depth in an organization. But what can be done to buck the trends noted by the Hay Group? One of the first and most important strategies is to be alert to signs of employee dissatisfaction that could lead to turnover. According to *Fortune* magazine, employees may signal dissatisfaction by disengaging from their work, being absent more frequently, and making more mistakes—all red flags that can result in turnover.[2] A leader who pays attention to such signs has a good chance of heading off problems and making changes that motivate a high-potential team player to remain.

Even better, however, is to encourage retention from the beginning by building in opportunities for team members to grow, learn, and advance within the organization instead of leaving it. Steve Geuther, former Florida sales director for the AmSan division of Interline Brands, had very little turnover among those who worked for him because he knew the value of supporting their growth, showing pathways to advancement, and creating a learning environment to foster depth.

One tactic that served Geuther well was to ask his high potentials to bring their résumés to their annual evaluations. Then he and the employees would have a personal discussion about what they had accomplished over the past year—updating the résumés in the process—and anticipate opportunities that might arise in the coming year. In doing this, Geuther not only showed his team that he was invested in them and wanted to see them succeed, but he also created an environment for them to learn, grow, and increase their professional value. The employees left the evaluations desiring to experience growth without leaving, and company retention became that much stronger.

Embracing internal competition can also be a driving force in employee retention, upward mobility, and innovation within the company. California Pizza Kitchen, a restaurant chain widely known for its creative takes on traditional recipes, has nearly three hundred locations in thirty-two US states and thirteen other countries, and its team members thrive off of its competitive learning culture. The organization created a "pizza chef program" in which pizza cooks can be certified by going through training in areas such as guest service, personality, and technical skills. When the process is complete, the cooks are rewarded with their own chef's coats and their names emblazoned on their working ovens.

But the opportunities don't end there. Certified pizza cooks are eligible to attend regional gatherings where they can share best practices, receive awards, and compete for the title of Best Pizza Chef. The competition is a sight to behold—the cooks enter the competition arena to theme music while hundreds of screaming fans (mostly friends, family, and coworkers) cheer them on in an unbelievable spirit of unity. The ultimate winners get their pizzas on the menu in their restaurants and a net award of twenty-five thousand dollars.

"Our people are our culture," said G. J. Hart, CEO. "So we developed this entire process to honor team members for their hard work."

GREAT TAKEAWAYS

Depth matters. Having a backup plan to replace essential personnel and develop others for future opportunities allows space for success on all fronts. Whether it involves encouraging healthy competition within an organization or training team members for advancement, building a deep team prepares for success against unforeseen obstacles.

While depth in the workplace is often restricted by an organization's financial capabilities—that is, not every organization can hire "extra" people—there is always the possibility of building depth using existing employees. As Brenton Hayden showcased at Renter's Warehouse, leaders can identify key backups and intentionally cultivate their talents. Such a plan not only prepares the company for the worst, but it also anticipates the best by providing the opportunity for more people to achieve greatness.

Leaders must take time to analyze whether their teams have the depth they need for success no matter the circumstances. They should also understand the impact that a particular member's departure—especially a high-performer—could have on the team. Great Teams have a plan for what happens when a starter is unable to perform. It's even a wise idea for an organization to build its own depth chart for when the inevitable happens. This begins by assessing bench strength and identifying high-potential team members who can take on roles during an emergency or transition. Those same high potentials should be challenged consistently in a company "employee combine"—an environment where employees can compete against each other for rewards or recognition—so that healthy competition can motivate team members to remain engaged. This also provides a better framework for decisions regarding employee promotions or replacements.

Team leaders should measure and possibly even display the results of the employee combine in order to keep track of performance. Like Anson Dorrance at UNC with his competitive cauldron, an organization can make the outcome of the competition public (at least within the company) so that high potentials know where they stand in relation to other team members. This will stoke competitive fires, which in turn will drive improvement and favorable results in the form of company success. However, leaders need to ensure that competition remains healthy by clarifying the boundaries and maintaining cooperation and unity so as not to create internal friction. Coach Shula of the Miami Dolphins encouraged competition among players in his team, but he never pitted his quarterbacks against each other in a way that allowed the competition to get personal.

Competitions provide an excellent opportunity for team leaders to promote a desire to get better. Leaders should praise winning employees for their good results, but they should also be mindful of finding ways to encourage improvement in poor-performing coworkers. Additionally, managers should emphasize improvement simply because the best players on a team want to grow, and backups need meaningful practices so that they are prepared to perform well.

Creating depth is not just a managerial concern but a responsibility that all must share. By providing an opportunity for employees to enhance their abilities and move their careers forward, a team's depth can help foster a culture of greatness.

CHAPTER 5

GREAT TEAMS HAVE A ROAD MAP

Their leaders build for the future with comprehensive plans.

Every Great Team lays out its plan for finding success in a clear and concise road map. To help navigate that vision, a successful organization has an active, well-designed training program with end goals in mind. This plan is the fabric of an organization's culture, and all involved in it understand the importance of following the road map to reach their desired success—even if the journey is a long one.

A road map guides a team in its pursuit of greatness and forms a culture in which individuals can identify their long-term roles. No team can achieve long-term success without one. Whether in the world of sports or business, a road map is vital to reaching a team's full potential.

GREAT TEAMS IN SPORTS

Coach Nick Saban arrived on the University of Alabama campus in 2007. His mission? Restoring prominence to a former national powerhouse.

Alabama's football program had declined significantly under the previous coach, who had lost four in a row to rival Auburn University and every road game of the 2006 season. The Crimson Tide was clearly in need of a jolt, so Alabama's athletic director sought out Saban and tasked him with returning Alabama to national relevance, just as he'd done with Louisiana State a few years earlier and as he had done at Michigan State before that.

Saban began his turnaround by introducing "the Process," his road map for developing greatness at all levels. He provided top-of-the-line support to his players by expanding academic aid and hiring a mental-toughness coach to help improve their competitive mind-sets. Saban's road map would assist in turning the program around, but more importantly, the Process was about focusing on the steps to achieve success and *not* fixating on the outcome itself. He stressed that he didn't want players focused on a championship as much as he wanted them focused on how they could get better today—could they do one more rep on the bench press, shave a fraction of a second off their sprint time, run a route closer to perfection, or add time to their studies to deliver better grades?

The Process wasn't reserved for players, either; Saban delivered detailed job descriptions to his staff, covering each person's exact role in the department and what would be expected of him or her on a daily basis.

Change wouldn't happen overnight. Alabama had a mediocre first year under Saban; the learning curve of a new defensive scheme and the Process proved to be too much of an adjustment. The Crimson Tide closed out the 2007 regular season with four straight losses, finishing 7–6. However, Saban remained committed to the Process, and the next year the team improved to 12–2. In 2009, two years after Saban took over as head coach, the Crimson Tide won the SEC championship game after defeating the number-one ranked Florida Gators, clinching an undefeated season and ultimately paving the way for a 37–21 win over Texas in the BCS national championship.

After that season, Alabama became the most powerful and consistent program in the college game, winning three championships over a four-year period. The Tide won a fourth championship in January 2016.

As former Alabama offensive coordinator Jim McElwain explained during an ESPN radio interview, Saban "has a vision. He has a plan. And yet, I think the thing that keeps him consistent and ahead of the curve, not just football-wise, but everything within the organization—there's a follow-up, as far as, 'What can we do better? What is new out there? What can we do, you know, to move things forward whether it is offense, defense, special teams, recruiting, academics, training room,' it doesn't matter. . . . What he does is set the vision and then gets great people around him and lets them be creative."[1]

Over the past few years, coaches from other schools have borrowed many of Saban's ideas. Florida State head coach Jimbo Fisher overhauled the nutrition program when he took over for Bobby Bowden, and former University of Texas coach Mack Brown made changes in his coaching staff after the 2010 season. Those moves were made with one eye looking at how Saban did his job with the Crimson Tide.

Long before he won ten NCAA men's basketball titles with his UCLA Bruins, Coach John Wooden developed his famous Pyramid of Success as a visual to instruct his players on how to win on the court and in life. The "blocks" of Wooden's pyramid were important attributes a winning player and a winning person must exemplify. The foundational bottom row included industriousness, friendship, loyalty, cooperation, and enthusiasm—key characteristics that everyone must embody. Stacked on top of these basics were upper-tier qualities such as self-control, initiative, skill, confidence, and poise. Wooden told his players to adopt each quality into their characters as they worked toward competitive greatness, which is the block at the top of the pyramid.

Competitive greatness, in Coach Wooden's mind, was reached when you were able to "be at your best when your best is needed."[2] To get there, he believed, you had to work through the blocks of the pyramid—and do so consistently.

Likewise, Bill Snyder, head coach of the Kansas State University Wildcats football team, installed a road map for his organization that transformed the struggling football program into a national powerhouse. When Snyder was hired to coach the Wildcats in 1989, the team had gone winless for two straight seasons. He didn't have a single player on his returning roster who had ever experienced a win at Kansas State. So one of the first things Snyder did to turn the team around was to post his "16 Goals for Success" as a motivator to inspire program change. These goals—gathered succinctly on a single page—were leadership terms with clearly spelled-out definitions—and expectations—for his players to follow daily. Snyder's 16 Goals were:

1. Commitment . . . to common goals and to being successful
2. Unselfishness . . . there is no "I" in team
3. Unity . . . come together as never before
4. Improve . . . every day as a player, person, and student
5. Be Tough . . . mentally and physically
6. Self-Discipline . . . do it right, don't accept less
7. Great Effort
8. Enthusiasm
9. Eliminate Mistakes . . . don't beat yourself
10. Never Give Up . . . never . . . never . . . never
11. Don't Accept Losing . . . if you do so one time, it will be easy to do so for the rest of your life
12. No Self-Limitations . . . expect more of yourself
13. Expect to Win . . . and truly believe we will
14. Consistency . . . your very, very best every time
15. Leadership . . . everyone can set the example
16. Responsibility . . . you are responsible for your performance[3]

Snyder asked his team to "think about these priorities for life" and to make a conscious effort to improve every one every single day.

"You have to put good ideas into play with your team," said Snyder. "Everyone on earth has set goals, but I'm a big believer of having a process. My message to young people was the ability to establish a process by which they could achieve whatever goals were significant and important in their lives."

The Wildcats used Snyder's clear vision as a driver, winning 193 victories in his twenty-four years of coaching. The turnaround of the Kansas State program—like Coach Wooden's turnaround at UCLA—proved the power of following and consistently applying a road map to chart a path to success.

Great Team cultures are often built in unexpected places and before the public takes notice. Having a road map is vital to bringing such a program out of relative obscurity. New York Giants general manager Jerry Reese, one of the sharpest men in his profession, has used this strategy to take his organization from an also-ran NFL team to two-time Super Bowl champions.

Reese chooses his coaches by asking about their plans—but not their game plans. "My first question would always be, 'Tell me about your off-season plan,'" he said. "Tell me where you plan to be in February, March, April, and May. The stuff you do in training camp—everybody knows how that works. The regular season—that's pretty well planned out already. What I want to know is how are you spending all that time you have to get ready for the season?"

Additionally, Reese said that his organization sees player development as part of that long-term vision. In 2004, the Giants traded to get quarterback Eli Manning, the number-one overall pick in the NFL Draft. While some quarterbacks start playing right away as rookies, the Giants had a specific plan for how to develop Manning. At the time the team was starting veteran quarterback Kurt Warner, and both Giants management and head coach Tom Coughlin wanted Manning to observe and shadow Warner carefully in order to get a sense of the job.

Just after the midpoint of the season, the team switched from Warner to Manning. At the time, some fans disagreed with the idea, citing that Manning was unprepared for the spotlight and would jeopardize the Giants' playoff hopes. However, Manning led the Giants to a strong regular season finish. He also improved dramatically as a leader and player over the next few years, leading the team to Super Bowl titles in 2007 and 2011.

For the Giants, Manning's development was one piece of an overall road map to victory.

AND FOR THE TRULY GREAT TEAMS IN BUSINESS

A Great Team outlines expectations for all members of an organization and for the organization as a whole. This clear-cut set of objectives—a road map—enables the organization to set benchmarks and goals and ultimately to lay the foundation for its own success.

Take, for example, Nestlé Global and its 4x4x4 Roadmap (also called the Nestlé Strategic Roadmap).[4] In this one-page document, Nestlé describes its vision for the brand across all departments and subsidiary products. This road map outlines Nestlé's four "competitive advantages," four "growth drivers," and four "operational pillars." Combined, these twelve principles form a clear outline of the company's plan for the future.

The Nestlé Strategic Roadmap differs from a typical business mission statement in the same way the plan of a successful sports organization differs from that of a mediocre one. Nestlé clearly states its goal to be "the leader in Nutrition, Health and Wellness, and the industry reference for financial performance, trusted by stakeholders."[5] Its road map spells out how it will achieve this goal as a company.

Nestlé isn't looking at just the desired result but at the steps required to get there. To illustrate this point, one of Nestlé's four growth drivers is "out-of-home consumption"[6]—one of the fastest growing segments of the food and beverage industry. Nestlé explains how it will target and cultivate this segment, stating that its company focus is on "added-value branded food and beverage solutions and services."[7]

Nestlé focuses on identifying potential pitfalls in its road map as well. One of its four competitive advantages is the "unmatched research and development capability" within the company. Again, Nestlé outlines the exact goal for this competitive advantage, which is "driving innovation and renovation that is relevant and attractive for consumers."[8] Nestlé's last competitive advantage in the food production industry is its corporate culture—undeniably why it has remained a global leader in food production.

A corporate road map should be nonnegotiable. That said, it should also be regularly revisited and updated due to the changing needs of the company and unexpected market forces. (Such is the nature of business.)

For Cheryl Bachelder, CEO of Popeyes Louisiana Kitchen, this reevaluation process proved difficult but necessary in order to continue moving the company forward.

After joining Popeyes in 2007, Bachelder crafted a "Roadmap to Results" in an effort to turn the company in a more profitable direction. She structured her vision around the company's four core business strategies: brand-building, running great restaurants, growing profits, and accelerating new unit growth. For four years Bachelder and her leadership team were tenacious in the application of their plan, until a board member suggested that maybe she was missing a few items in her long-term vision.

Bachelder resisted the thought of shifting direction, but the feedback of the Popeyes board member was enough to prompt her to revisit her established road map. After careful analysis, Bachelder realized that they were, indeed, missing two important objectives: 1) a proposition centered on friendlier customer service, and 2) a stronger approach to developing a people-centered culture.

With the Roadmap to Results updated and the two new focuses added, Popeyes grew its market share, improved guest ratings, and increased restaurant margins both in the United States and abroad. In the last six years, the enterprise market cap increased from three hundred million to more than a billion dollars.

Bachelder says that if a team clings too stubbornly to its corporate road map, it can become complacent and may miss the warnings that signal a reevaluation may be in order. Leaders must remain objective enough to acknowledge progress with a grain of salt and be willing to tweak their plans, knowing that what made them good won't always make them great.

"The leader has a responsibility to come up above the trees periodically and refresh the vision and make sure they've looked at the landscape as if they've never seen it before," said Bachelder in an interview for *Leadercast Now*.[9] Great Teams who do this can manage adapting to change and updating the road map to compensate for the growing needs of the organization.

A road map also allows a team to plan on managing future company growth and use it as leverage to move into new areas of business. Since its creation in 2004, tech juggernaut and global sensation Facebook continues to take the market by storm, and with each passing year it shows no sign of slowing down. In 2014 alone, the company earned an incredible $12.5 billion.[10]

Though business is presently booming, CEO Mark Zuckerberg envisions a future where Facebook is a global leader in the next technological revolution—and he has a three-, five-, and ten-year road map to get there.

"We're going to prepare for the future by investing aggressively in it," Zuckerberg said, as quoted in an article for *Business Insider*.[11]

One of Zuckerberg's major three-year goals is to continue investing heavily in video production, advertising (which includes the improvement of targeting and launching new platforms to reach people across devices), and pushing for more timely, relevant, and public content.

Over the next five years, he plans to build up the business acumen to connect billions of people with next-generation versions of Instagram, WhatsApp, Search, and Messenger. A vital part of Facebook's strategy during this period will be to help developers construct, grow, and ultimately monetize their apps across major mobile platforms. Currently, Facebook has more than 1.5 million advertisers, and by connecting with app developers for monetization, that number will grow.

Ten years from now, Zuckerberg hopes to have fundamentally changed the world with artificial intelligence and developed next-generation computing. Presently, Facebook has completed construction of Aquila—a solar-powered unmanned drone capable of beaming down Internet connectivity—as part of its Internet.org effort to connect even the most remote regions of the planet.

Instead of keeping the company's ambitious goals confined to top executives, Zuckerberg has invited contribution and criticism from his employees by freely sharing Facebook's road map. Such transparency is literally embedded in the company's culture; at the company's Palo Alto headquarters, employees work in large open areas rather than being confined in offices, and boardrooms are encased in glass.

"We want to create this very open and transparent culture in our company where . . . everyone can see what everyone else is working on," said Zuckerberg in a video tour of those offices. "We think that this facilitates this very open and transparent culture, which again enables us to do our best work."[12]

GREAT TAKEAWAYS

A road map gives a company a plan to achieve its collective goals. As with Nestlé's 4x4x4 Roadmap, this plan should both outline a capable vision of an organization's future and anticipate how the company can achieve its goals.

A good road map increases efficiency and streamlines organizational focus through clarity. It outlines team members' responsibilities and provides an opportunity to ingrain the organization's culture into its workforce. Like Saban's Process, Wooden's Pyramid, or Snyder's 16 Goals, a road map outlines the path to success and motivates the players to achieve greatness.

So how does an organization build an effective road map? Leaders can start by identifying members of the team who can help with instituting the long-term goals. Dictating responsibility early will help a team stay organized during major initiatives. Next, management should identify the various goals the team is working toward. By determining which goals need their own clearly defined road maps, the leaders can then create daily steps toward achieving them.

Second, an organization must plan for detours along the way. Obstacles will happen—there's no avoiding them—and management should plan for ways to continue moving forward. As Popeyes Louisiana Kitchen demonstrated, constant reviews and updates to the road map are inevitable and necessary when responding to the changing needs of the company.

Additionally, as Mark Zuckerberg's Facebook has shown, leaders should take steps to ensure that the road map is engrained at all levels of the culture so employees will be motivated by the direction of the team.

High-performing organizations have visionary, engaging road maps. These tools go beyond simple mission statements; they are active, clear, and actionable objectives that lead to success. All employees understand the important components, know their places within the road map, and can take defined steps each day to achieve greatness together within their organizations.

CHAPTER 6

GREAT TEAMS PROMOTE CAMARADERIE AND A SENSE OF COLLECTIVE DIRECTION

Their members develop a sense of responsibility through fellowship.

Team building requires buy-in among all members to what the collective direction and goals of the company are supposed to be. In other words, it requires camaraderie—fellowship among members of the team.

Camaraderie doesn't happen by accident; developing a strong sense of trust, accountability, and togetherness around team goals requires intentional effort. When an organization comes to a collective understanding of its objective, the individuals develop a sense of responsibility to each other. They know the direction the team is heading and trust that their teammates are willing to work hard to accomplish their respective goals. This chapter will explore what some of the Great Teams in sports and business have done to promote camaraderie and a sense of collective direction among their members.

GREAT TEAMS IN SPORTS

If ever a team needed a better sense of collective direction, it was the 2013 Boston Red Sox. During the 2012 season, the team had finished 69–93, last place in the American League East—the first time the Sox had more than ninety losses since 1966. As a result, Red Sox owner John Henry made wholesale changes to the organization by releasing manager Bobby Valentine and hiring Toronto Blue Jays manager John Farrell as his replacement. The organization made changes to its roster as well, adding veterans David Ross, Jonny Gomes, and Mike Napoli.

Ross, a backup catcher for the Atlanta Braves, had been at the top of Boston's off-season wish list—but not primarily for his on-field performance. Though a talented player, he was signed because of his presence in the clubhouse. Ross was a natural leader and the type of player who drew the attention of others. And unlike some voices in the 2012 locker room, he was a positive influence. His goals were aligned with the goals of the ownership, and the rest of the players tended to follow his lead.

Before the Red Sox began the 2013 season, Henry and Farrell assembled the players and informed them that the organization would do whatever it took to ensure their success. If these players felt the Red Sox weren't giving them something they needed to succeed, Henry said, they should speak up, and it would be provided.

"Ownership was like, 'We want to give you everything you need so you can best perform on that field,'" said Ross. "I knew then that in tough times, the front office had my back."

In essence, the Red Sox owners were telling the players that the roles would be reversed—that the owners were available for the players as a resource and not the other way around. Henry and company wanted to give the team members every opportunity to play their best baseball. Just knowing that inspired a sense of mutual trust and camaraderie in the team members, Ross said.

Camaraderie developed in the clubhouse as well. At spring training, new outfielder Gomes arrived at practice unshaven. The other newcomers, Napoli and Ross, immediately followed suit and began growing out their beards. As the team won its way through the season, the beards became as identifiable with the Red Sox as their red-striped uniforms. As the beards grew, players started tugging on them as a way to acknowledge success, and fans started wearing makeshift beards to games.

The beards were just one example of the sense of brotherhood growing within team ranks. The entire team began taking the early bus to games together and sitting together for meals. Teammates talked together a lot too—encouraging each other and revving each other up to do their best.

Though an eleven-year veteran, Ross remarked that he had never seen a team talk as much about the World Series as this team. It was a common response to a greeting. One player would say, "How are you?" and his teammate would respond, "Another day closer to the World Series."

Even as the 2013 Red Sox were building a strong sense of camaraderie and shared purpose inside the clubhouse, a tragedy outside the franchise strengthened team resolve. The horrific bombing at the finish line of that year's Boston Marathon gripped the city in a panic and, in the aftermath of the attack, created an entirely new sense of direction for the team. The Red Sox believed they were playing not only for their fans but also for the city of Boston itself. Players frequently visited victims in the hospital and hosted first responders in the dugout, all with the intention of lifting the spirits of the community—the city and everyone whose lives were forever changed by that moment of terrorism.

After the April 15 bombings, the team's quest for a championship evolved into something much stronger: players were keenly aware of playing for the healing of their city. Team goals now took on new importance, with each player holding himself and his teammates accountable for not letting the team, the franchise, or the city down.

Since camaraderie arises from a sense of collective direction and fosters both drive and teamwork, the 2013 Red Sox quickly found themselves on the path to success. Leadership in the clubhouse mirrored the goals of the coaches. The team members agreed not only on their goal but also on how to achieve it. And achieve they did. Under the new leadership of John Farrell and the recruits, the Red Sox won the 2013 World Series.

The team's sudden improvement from worst to first happened as a result of a renewed sense of camaraderie in the dugout and helped a competitive baseball team become an unstoppable team bonded by beards, accountability, and support.

The San Antonio Spurs not only have a dynamic team culture and a strong, evolving road map to success, but they also have been exceedingly successful in developing camaraderie through open communication. Head coach Gregg Popovich has created a platform that involves everyone—from the management team to the players—in the execution and development of strategic game planning and decisions. Spurs leaders are upfront with all incoming players and staff on the team's philosophy of communication and transparency.

"There is an expectation to be prepared when you come in to our organization to have a voice," said R. C. Buford, general manager of the Spurs. "It puts people in a framework where they can communicate and grow. When people arrive and are engaged, they are thrown into an environment of participation."

One of the best examples of this open line of communication was demonstrated in 2011, when Spurs management made the decision to trade George Hill, a favorite among players and coaches, to the Indiana Pacers for the draft rights to Kawhi Leonard. Because Hill was so beloved in the locker room, there was great angst from both coaches and players when the trade was being considered. But then, once the decision was made, the Spurs committed as a unit to the strategic decision to move forward.

"We argue out these decisions, and because people have been included in the process, hopefully they understand that we can't execute every strategy that everyone comes in with," said Buford. "There is a great deal of emotion that goes with a team environment, but at the end of the day, agree or disagree, we are going to commit."

Leonard has proven the wisdom of management's choice, developing into the next great star on the Spurs roster and winning Finals MVP after the team won the NBA Championship in 2014.

An open line of communication is a hallmark for a Great Team, and the Spurs certainly demonstrate that, but they are equally masterful at creating camaraderie among very diverse players. The Spurs have consistently built a team with world-class, international talent, which management uses to create a competitive advantage. In the case of breakout star and backup point guard Patty Mills, the Spurs have rallied around his unique background to further instill brotherhood.

Mills is an indigenous Australian, a Torres Strait Islander, and every June 3 recognizes "Eddie Mabo Day," a commemorative day celebrating the Australian government's decision to grant land rights to the indigenous. For Mills and his countrymen, the day is as important as the Fourth of July is to Americans. In 2014, while the Spurs were watching game film in preparation for an NBA Finals game that would be played two days later, Coach Popovich called on Mills to explain what Mabo Day meant to him. After Mills finished, his teammates gave him a round of applause.

"It was unbelievable," Mills said in an article for the *San Antonio Express-News*. "I had no idea Pop was going to do it. I had no idea he even knew about [Mabo Day], but for him to bring that up in a meeting before the NBA finals, just to give everyone a heads-up, was very special."[1]

Popovich's gesture was compellingly thoughtful but also very wise, considering its success in building camaraderie in the Spurs' culture. Popovich stopped game preparation because he wanted a member of his team to share who he was and where he was from. The Spurs were able to learn more about their teammate and to channel his experience into motivation, which may ultimately have helped them win the 2014 NBA championship. Popovich's simple request created an immediate bond among the Spurs, strengthening the team culture in the process.

As the Boston Red Sox beards indicated, symbols can contribute powerfully to a team's camaraderie. They can carry a team toward unprecedented levels of focus and success. Just before their championship-winning run in the 2015 NCAA tournament, Coach Krzyzewski and the Duke Blue Devils signed a special ball with the names of loved ones, motivators, and influencers in each of their lives.

"The names represented everyone who has made it possible for us to be in the tournament at that moment," said Krzyzewski, who wrote down seven names himself. "We said that after we won it all, we would send an autographed ball from all of us to each of the people on the special ball and explain to them the significant impact they had upon our lives."

Similarly, St. Louis Cardinals' chairman Bill DeWitt and his management team send a sixty-eight-page book to all new recruits. The book is packed with historical relevancies, general expectations for a Cardinal player, and specific instructions tailored to that particular player's position. The information is helpful, but it is the book itself that carries the meaning of "now you're one of us."

"It's important to have all staff on the same page, from top to bottom," said DeWitt. "The book itself is a good tool, but it really is the people who find the meaning within it and put it into practice."

Sylvia Hatchell, head coach of the women's basketball team at the University of North Carolina at Chapel Hill, is the third-winningest head coach in NCAA women's basketball history. She has built a strong team culture by creating a family system and promoting a mentality of respect and winning—especially in regards to developing camaraderie.

"You take your two best players, and if they are not on the same page then you aren't going to win," Hatchell shared with me. "And it's just as important to have chemistry as a team. I've won championships at the AIAW, NAIA and the NCAA, and they weren't always my most talented teams, but they were great because of chemistry."

Hatchell boosts team chemistry by presenting tongue depressors to her players, staff, and trainers, who are then told to personalize the wooden sticks according to each individual's personality, style of play, and devotion to team. Then she has them bundle all of the sticks together and picks a volunteer to try to break them—an impossible task. "The message of the tongue depressors is that strength and unity [equals] togetherness," Hatchell said. "Out there by yourself, you can be broken. With your team, you can't. That's how you win championships."

The sticks became a fixture in the culture of the team and helped turn the tide of the 1994 national championship game. The Lady Tar Heels were down by two with seven-tenths of a second left and, during the huddle, several players retrieved their sticks so that the team could rally around the inspirational messages. Utilizing the sticks at a crucial moment reminded the team of their collective mission and their winning mentality. Ultimately, the Lady Tar Heels won the game with a perfectly orchestrated buzzer beater—in part because the players were reminded that they could accomplish anything if they all played together.

AND FOR THE TRULY GREAT TEAMS IN BUSINESS

Colonel Bernie Banks, department head for West Point's Department of Behavioral Sciences and Leadership, describes the practice of intentionally developing a collective direction and camaraderie in a team as *colaperation*. This coined term covers the entire process of fostering a cooperative environment, soliciting buy-ins from team members, "having a clear vision of where you are trying to take people," and "establishing a coalition to move forward."

"Colaperation is cooperation and collaboration together," said Banks. "So you are trying to foster [not only] a cooperative environment, but also one where people are openly collaborating. I find that high-performance organizations really foster this notion of colaperation; you are going to push me and I am going to push you, but we are doing it together."

Banks's example is congruent with an emphasis evident across many educational institutions—especially business schools. These schools stress that students are present to help one another to learn, but that in order for the learning to happen, they'll have to push each other as well.

"Organizations with multiple departments should desire to push themselves to be the best that they can," said Banks. "Clearly, others are going to compete in a certain sense, but never in a way that will not reflect a sincere desire to cooperate with peers."

Michael Lee Stallard, president of E Pluribus Partners and world expert on corporate camaraderie, says that Great Teams are inevitably "connection cultures." Stallard believes that connection is one of the most essential elements in an organization, no matter what the field. Building mental and emotional bridges among team members can increase employee engagement, productivity, and innovation.

"Humans have a biological need to feel connected," Stallard said. "Furthermore, an employee's feelings of connection, community, and unity are the most powerful and least understood aspects of successful organizations."[2]

It's easy to see that camaraderie in a corporate team can carry it through the trenches as everyone marches toward a shared destination. But what does camaraderie really look like in a corporate setting, and what can be created when deep connections are fostered?

Memorial Sloan Kettering Cancer Institute, one of the best cancer treatment facilities in the world, provides an incredible case study on the power of connection in an organization. A cancer diagnosis is a frightening one, but from the moment patients walk through the doors of Memorial Sloan Kettering, they are greeted by Nick Medley, the "hugger and healer" doorman who embraces patients as if they are long-lost family members. (A cancer survivor himself, in a sense he *is* a family member.) Nick remembers the patients' names and their diagnoses and does his best to provide them with hope and joy as they endure their treatments.

And the connection doesn't stop there. The connection culture at MSK ensures that everyone from security to administrative staff welcomes patients with great warmth and caring. Memorial Sloan Kettering strongly believes in the healing power of encouragement, optimism, and an upbeat mood. Working together, the staff is able to transform a grim time of life into one of empowerment and togetherness, making every patient's fight against cancer their own as well.[3]

Stallard recognizes the power of such a culture, which cannot develop without a commitment from management. "A leader can create a connection culture by sharing vision, value, and voice. When that leader communicates an inspiring vision and lives it, values others and gives them a voice, they feel connected. If all three are recognized, then the byproduct is a great organizational culture."[4]

The Ford Motor Company knows better than anyone that developing a connection culture can turn around the fate of an organization and truly make the difference between success and failure—even when rebounding from the brink of collapse. The company was struggling in 2006, when CEO Alan Mulally sought to create a stronger organizational culture. By communicating Henry Ford's original vision of putting America to work with affordable transportation, Mulally connected his employees with a greater purpose and gave them a voice to contribute their opinions. The mission drove the design, and Ford not only recovered but produced new designs and affordable development. By diverting the focus away from the fears of brand failure and instead pointing both its customers and its workforce to a reliable product and brand confidence, the company was able to fight back—as a team.

Ford recovered its culture and business goals, reconnecting the vision between company and consumer—and proving the truth of what Stallard said: "Caring about people is the most important value in leadership. True leadership cares about others and results. Ultimately, the results are benefiting people."[5]

GREAT TAKEAWAYS

As the Boston Red Sox, Memorial Sloan Kettering, Ford Motor Company, and the UNC–Chapel Hill Women's basketball team demonstrated, the key to developing a collective sense of direction is building a structure of togetherness. To get employees on the same page with one another, companies must reach beyond the individual and truly connect.

In the case of the 2013 World Series champion Red Sox, the ownership took steps to align the individual desires of the players with the franchise's overall goal. The players knew their goal and talked about it relentlessly. They even grew unsightly facial hair as a constant reminder. This symbolic act helped build a stronger connection among players and create an environment ripe for accountability and determination.

Helping players buy in to a collective direction can improve a team's chemistry and focus on and off the field. Ideally team members will develop personal bonds that heighten their senses of responsibility to maintain the team's direction.

Leaders should aspire to create camaraderie because it facilitates trust in the collective direction for their organizations. It all begins, as R. C. Buford said, with maintaining an open line of communication. Leadership teams have to declare what they are trying to build by having honest conversations and alerting everyone of their goals. Great managers also believe in their teams; they know their employees are capable of the work expected of them and then trust that the employees will actually complete those tasks.

Great leaders actively seek the places, events, causes, and exercises where they can unify their teams behind constructive practices; it's the constant practice of reinforcing culture. Many Great Teams bond in moments away from the workplace. A team can set aside time to create these bonds and camaraderie—through a company lunch, charity work, or even a fantasy football league—further solidifying and maintaining enjoyment and engagement. These gestures could have a phenomenal impact and not only bring a team together but strengthen the pursuit of a common goal.

Camaraderie is often overlooked, but it can be the greatest asset in unifying a team. Organizations should value fellowship as a competitive advantage that not only recruits A-caliber employees but improves engagement, productivity, and retention.

Pillar Three

ACTIVATING EFFICIENCY

CHAPTER 7

GREAT TEAMS MANAGE DYSFUNCTION, FRICTION, AND STRONG PERSONALITIES

They know how to succeed despite adversity and friction.

While 100 percent camaraderie is the dream scenario for team culture, some degree of dysfunction is likely in even the best situations. When a team has strong personalities and talented people, there will inevitably be friction. Great Team leaders know how to manage friction and personality conflicts to keep challenges from derailing the team's success.

In this chapter we will consider examples of how some Great Teams handled dysfunction by promoting cultures in which the members were motivated to appreciate their respective values to the teams' overall goals even though they didn't always like one another.

In order to resolve conflict between team members effectively, it helps to have an understanding of how such conflict typically develops. In the 1960s, psychiatrist Stephen Karpman developed a helpful model for such understanding. Popularly known as the Karpman Drama Triangle, this model reveals the way that people involved in an interpersonal conflict tend to cast themselves in one of three basic roles—victims, persecutors, or rescuers. These roles are a general description of the way a participant behaves in a disagreement. Note that the roles are specific to the conflict. That is, the same person might play a different role in a different situation.

The "victims" role is perhaps the easiest to understand. Victims are the people who feel forced to give in or give up when faced with conflict. They believe (or at least assume) that giving in to the persecutor's demands would be easier than facing conflict. Some may even take satisfaction in sacrifice or secretly enjoy the victim role.

The "persecutors," on the other hand, are the individuals who tend to force their own agendas and pressure the victim types to give in to demands or ideas.

"Rescuers" are likely to intervene on behalf of the victims, arguing against the persecutors' ideas. Rescuers are not necessarily looking out for the victims, however. They are often motivated by a desire to force an alternate agenda or the personal satisfaction of fighting the fight.

The roles of persecutor, victim, and rescuer are played out in disagreements in sports and business each and every day. Such a clash of personalities can heavily disrupt the productivity of a team—or can even destroy it. But if the situation is handled wisely, the fireworks can be defused and a productive working relationship can move forward on a more positive note.

GREAT TEAMS IN SPORTS

Six-time Sprint Cup Series champion Jimmie Johnson is one of the most successful drivers in NASCAR and has built a career that many only dream of. Johnson, in his No. 48 Chevrolet SS, has won more than seventy races for Hendrick Motorsports—including the Budweiser Shootout, Coca-Cola 600, and Brickyard 400—and is a six-time Driver of the Year, the most in the history of the award. But in 2005, long before most of these accomplishments, he and long-time crew chief Chad Knaus came close to splitting apart due to a clash of egos. The arguments ranged from work ethic to attitude to dedication, and the combination came close to destroying Team 48.

"Chad and I were just on each other—very short fuses, talking aggressively to one another," Johnson told me. "I guess to an outsider listening in we were acting like kids, like brats, just fighting with each other over petty things. Our desire to succeed was so great that anything that would normally have been a one on your frustration scale was a ten on ours. Everything was an explosion. We were just going through the motions at the track. I was communicating what I felt with the car. He was responding back. But we were using as few words as possible. Our sport is so people-based that energy and vibe—that dynamic—is very real for us. At that time, everything felt off."

But team boss and owner Rick Hendrick refused to see his team fail. He called a surprise meeting between Johnson and Knaus, who were barely speaking at the time.

When the two men arrived in Hendrick's office, they found what looked like a scene straight out of an elementary school. A table had been set with a huge batch of cookies, some Mickey Mouse plates, and a couple of liters of milk. As the two bewildered men looked to Hendrick for an explanation, he told them that if they were going to act like children, then he'd treat them both as such.

"Hendrick basically told us that nobody was leaving the room until everybody had been honest with themselves," said Johnson.

Knaus and Johnson ate the milk and cookies while they hashed out everything on their respective minds—ultimately opening up the lines of communication. Their bristling egos relaxed into a shared understanding of each other's perspective.

One of their disagreements, for instance, had centered on how to fine-tune Johnson's car. Johnson had wanted it to be more controllable, and Knaus, like most crew chiefs, had wanted it to be faster. As they spoke the men realized that what both of them wanted more than anything was to win. That shared desire could be a basis for productive teamwork.

The milk-and-cookies conversation facilitated by Hendrick for Knaus and Johnson is fascinating because it perfectly demonstrates the Karpman Drama Triangle. Johnson and Knaus each viewed himself as the victim and the other person as the persecutor—and ultimately

Hendrick had to step in as the rescuer. More important, this story represents a pivotal moment in the history of Team 48—the moment when its leaders decided to put ego aside to connect over a shared vision of winning. The meeting helped both Knaus and Johnson understand the importance of openly communicating with one another rather than internalizing slights and disagreements, which can grow into grudges that erode a team from the inside.

"That was definitely a starting point because for the first time in a while, we actually talked," Johnson said. "Chad opened up and shared stress factors he was facing. I did too. We both admitted that we had been pushing each other's hot buttons."

Johnson and Knaus still have differences and disagree, but as any Great Team members do, they've figured out how to debate with the larger goal in mind, knowing this larger goal is more important than their own individual desires. Both have found they complement each other well—Johnson with his incredible feel for driving and Knaus with his technical and mechanical talent—and they are almost always ahead of the competition. By properly managing conflict and dysfunction, the two men have developed into a formidable team.

And it all began with a table full of milk and cookies—and a leader who wasn't going to let dysfunction ruin a Great Team.

Great Teams understand the reasons behind conflict and find ways to rise above it; however, conflict resolution is a skill that must be exercised to be effective. Unfortunately, no matter the talent of the individuals, competing egos can disrupt even the most successful of organizations.

Future NBA Hall of Famers Kobe Bryant and Shaquille O'Neal played together for eight years on the Los Angeles Lakers (1996–2004) and were instrumental in three of the Lakers' eleven NBA championships. The combination of O'Neal's formidable physical presence with Bryant's scoring and ball-handling skills proved unstoppable. But behind the dominance, a well-documented feud was brewing.

As Bryant began to position himself as the future of the franchise, O'Neal held firmly to his role as team leader, putting the two personalities on an inevitable collision course. Their backgrounds before joining the Lakers couldn't have been more different. O'Neal was a rising star for the Orlando Magic and Bryant an elite high school standout. But their histories contained a common thread—each player came from a system designed to get the ball into his hands. And Phil Jackson's triangle offense could only run through one of them—usually O'Neal.

For a while Bryant ran the offense as designed, but tension between the two stars began to build when he began to take more offensive control. In 1999 O'Neal confronted Bryant in a team meeting, saying Bryant was playing too selfishly for the team to win. Bryant disputed this statement but continued to play his role in the offense, and the Lakers won the title for that year—and the next.

Eventually, the feud between O'Neal and Bryant moved from the locker room to the media room. Bryant told reporters he did not think the Lakers' offense was conducive to his abilities. Then he took it upon himself to score more, eventually taking offensive possessions from O'Neal. Despite this friction between their two superstars, however, the Lakers tore through the regular season and swept the New Jersey Nets for their third title.

In any other organization, conflict between the star players probably would not have resulted in championship-winning play. But luckily the Lakers management, specifically head coach Phil Jackson and general manager Jerry West, knew how to handle their strong personalities well enough to keep their team from faltering. Team leadership clearly communicated that they would not allow the demands of Bryant or O'Neal to derail the season—and for a time, it worked.

The two continued to trade barbs through the press and refused to acknowledge each other outside of team activities. In 2003, assistant coach Brian Shaw had to separate the two players in practice when another disagreement threatened to become a fistfight.

The situation was quickly becoming untenable. The feud between

Bryant and O'Neal had the potential to destroy the Lakers' shot at ever winning the title again. Neither player wanted to compromise on his vision for the team's offense or on his desire to be the team's leader.

After the 2004 season the Lakers traded O'Neal to the Miami Heat, with whom he won an NBA title in 2006. Bryant, on the other hand, was given an extension to remain with the Lakers. With the Lakers offense now revolving around him, Bryant and his team won two more NBA titles—in 2009 and 2010.

In retrospect, Bryant and O'Neal were both partially right. Each one *was* capable of leading a championship team. Unfortunately, the drive to lead was more personal for the two players, and with each refusing to bend to the other's will, the entire team suffered. If not for the Lakers management playing the "rescuer" role and eliciting a compromise between Bryant and O'Neal, however temporary, their effectiveness as a team would have been greatly diminished.

Team management must be strong in the event of conflict among players, but what if the conflict is between the coaches? If the leadership of a team is feuding, the tension will trickle down to every level of the organization—unless the team itself, empowered by the culture of the institution, refutes the negativity.

The 1985 Chicago Bears are one of the most storied teams in the history of the NFL. Featuring Hall of Famers Walter Payton, Richard Dent, Dan Hampton, Mike Singletary, and head coach Mike Ditka, the team went 15–1 and rolled to a victory in the Super Bowl behind its ferocious defense, dubbed "The Monsters of the Midway." The organization was full of great players with even bigger personalities, such as quarterback Jim McMahon and defensive lineman William "The Refrigerator" Perry. This special group was both talented and tough, and its defense set numerous NFL records, including fewest points allowed in a season.

The wild side of the team also extended to its coaches. Ditka and defensive coordinator Buddy Ryan were no-nonsense, tough-talking coaches. Bears fans loved their fiery attitudes and snarling approaches to leadership. But behind the scenes, Ditka and Ryan didn't work well together.

The problem began at the outset of Ditka's tenure in 1982, when he was hired by legendary Bears founder and owner George Halas. Ryan had been with Chicago since 1978, when Halas hired him to work with new head coach Neill Armstrong to tighten up the defense.

Ryan had impressed the Bears with his work around the NFL, including stints with the rival Minnesota Vikings and the New York Jets. His defense had played a pivotal role in the Jets' historic upset of the Baltimore Ravens in the 1968 Super Bowl. And after four years as defensive coordinator for the Bears, Ryan felt he'd earned the head coaching position. He was shocked when Halas overlooked him in favor of Ditka.

To complicate matters even more, Halas ordered Ditka to keep Ryan. Because of this decision, Ryan knew that Ditka had very little power over him, so he would openly disagree with Ditka in practice and at times even disregard his directives.

When Ditka joined the team, Ryan was in the midst of developing a new blitz-happy scheme known as the 46 defense, which freed the Bears' hyperathletic linebackers to attack the offense from a variety of directions. The 46 defense was Ryan's brainchild, and he would not let Ditka determine how it would be managed. In a November 1985 game against the Dallas Cowboys—the team Ditka had coached as an assistant before coming to Chicago—Ryan set out to prove to Ditka and Ditka's former employer the true dominance of this new defensive scheme.

After three quarters, the Bears had built a 27–0 lead. To avoid embarrassing head coach Tom Landry and the Cowboys, Ditka instructed Ryan to back off—but Ryan refused. In fact, he called for more blitzes and aggressive coverage on the Cowboys' receivers. Chicago ultimately won 44–0, handing Dallas its worst defeat in franchise history and its first shutout defeat in fifteen years.

At that point, the tension between the coaches and even their respective players had reached a boiling point. Practices between the offense and defense became more competitive than ever, and players had a hard time getting along with one another.

Finally, two weeks after the Dallas game, the tension reached a breaking point. Playing on a Monday night in Miami, Chicago was 12–0 and trying to match Miami's undefeated season from 1972. But the Dolphins and Coach Don Shula were prepared for the showdown, even bringing members of the 1972 team to the game to stand on the sidelines to help amp both the team and the crowd.

Even though the Bears had the 46 defense, superstar players, and lots of swagger, their internal conflict unraveled everything in the Miami game. Shula's plan was a perfect antidote for what Chicago was doing, and the Dolphins had built a twenty-point lead by halftime. At the break, Ditka and Ryan had to be physically separated in the Chicago locker room. Ditka instructed Ryan in the first half to drop back into coverage on defense instead of continuing to attack. But once again Ryan refused to back down, fully believing in the strength of his defense.

The Bears mounted a comeback but ultimately fell short as the Dolphins recorded a 38–24 win, crushing the Bears' hopes for an undefeated season. The conflict and lack of respect between Ryan and Ditka was obvious, and news of the near-fistfight spread quickly through the media after the Bears' loss.

With tensions high, the players had to find a way to coexist for the remainder of the season. Fortunately, one of the team's players had agreed weeks earlier that the players would film a video that became known as the "Super Bowl Shuffle." The video was a comical rap song that the team audaciously released before the actual Super Bowl. The goal was to raise money for the Chicago Community Trust, which provided clothes, food, and shelter to needy families in the city, but it accomplished something else too.

In the video, Singletary, Payton, and Willie Gault danced and rapped while McMahon donned sunglasses and a serious demeanor. Backup quarterback Steve Fuller also created a sense of comic relief because of his lack of dancing and rap skills. The frivolous, hilarious day created a unique bonding experience for the team, melting the conflict that had seeped down from the clashing coaching staff.

Singletary credited the video shoot of the "Super Bowl Shuffle" as the catalyst that "solved the conflict" of the team. Ultimately, the Bears went on to win the actual Super Bowl that year, cementing their legacy as one of the best NFL teams of all time. And in a rare show of dual loyalty, the players carried both Ditka and Ryan off the field after the game.

Ryan and Ditka never came to terms. Ryan was hired as the head coach for the Philadelphia Eagles in 1986, and the feuding continued at a distance. Ryan was never shy about mocking both the Bears and their coach. And after a Bears-Eagles matchup in 1989, Ditka famously responded by saying, "You know what they say. Empty tin cans make the most noise, and he's an empty tin can."[1]

Within the Bears organization, however, the tension generated by the conflict between the coaches was resolved by the players. What it took was doing something fun and—most importantly—together.

AND FOR THE TRULY GREAT TEAMS IN BUSINESS

In any industry or sport, some degree of internal conflict is inevitable. Personality differences are amplified when individuals work long hours alongside one another and rivalry is encouraged within an organization.

The world of sports is a perfect example of this dynamic. Players are in direct competition for playing time, endorsements, and money. But it's also a factor in the business world, where up-and-coming employees compete for jobs with established employees. And in both sports and business, disagreements about work and plain old personality conflicts can increase tension even in noncompetitive situations.

Too often, office drama reduces team productivity, collaboration, and morale. It can also be expensive. Internal friction is one of the greatest expense items for companies. According to the *CPP Global Human*

Capital Report, 25 percent of employees were so upset by the idea of facing a workplace conflict that they called in sick or were absent from work. Additionally, 10 percent of those surveyed reported that a project failed as a result of negative conflict, and more than a third said negative conflict resulted in someone leaving the company. Employees in American businesses said they spent 2.8 hours per week dealing with conflict, which amounts to $359 billion in paid hours, an indication that conflict is eating American organizations up from the inside.[2]

That's not to say that all conflict in the workplace is bad. The common perception is that conflict should be avoided at all costs. But not all conflict is negative or deconstructive. It can be a source of tremendous energy and innovation when managed well. But managing it well is no easy task.

According to the Thomas-Kilmann Conflict Mode Instrument, leaders commonly manage—or mismanage—conflict in one of five ways.[3]

Some rely on their rank and title, debating fiercely if necessary, to force their way through workplace friction. That's *competing.*

Others try to "play nice," giving in to even unreasonable demands to keep the peace. Their strategy is *accommodating.*

Some fail at addressing conflict because they'd rather pretend it isn't happening and hope it will settle itself. They are masters at *avoiding* the issues.

Still others prefer *compromising* and try for a middle ground.

Each of these four strategies for dealing with conflict can have some success. But Great Teams set a standard above the rest by choosing the fifth option—*collaborating.* This means they do their best to listen actively, consider all points of view, and stress the common purpose and shared values of the organization.

Jenn Lim, CEO and CHO (Chief Happiness Officer) of Delivering Happiness—a science-based firm that promotes happiness, passion, and purpose at work—uses a "happiness survey" to determine employee engagement, and she believes that a shared purpose is the key to employee satisfaction.

"It is so important to align the individual's purpose with the company because even the person doing the most remedial job won't think of things as a task, but they will think of it as part of their career," she shared. "Anyone who walks through the door should think that they are the reason why the company exists."

The leaders of Great Teams in sports and business would agree with Lim. To avoid conflict, it's important that values not only be shared but also acknowledged. And when trouble appears, seasoned leaders know to step in at the right moment, before conflict takes hold, to assert compromise and positive collaboration. Friction will always be a possibility, but a Great Team should also be ready to utilize collaboration so as not to lose momentum.

Through the 1990s, global manufacturer of computer technology IBM was in the process of reorganizing itself—combining independent divisions, sales divisions, and delivery divisions—with the goal of providing solutions, bundled products, and effective services to its customers. This reintegration created complexities and friction among IBM's senior management matrix. Cross-unit issues developed as managers failed to coordinate with one another, escalating conflicts and straining relationships across the leadership level.[4]

IBM executives immediately addressed the growing disagreements and ultimately created the Market Growth Workshop, an internal forum dedicated to resolving issues by encouraging cooperation and collaboration of its cross-unit managers. Once a month IBM's management, sales teams, and frontline employees would connect over a conference call to discuss and resolve conflicts so that workplace friction would not hinder customer support or sales. The organization's culture of always meeting the needs of the customer took precedence over internal strife, and the forum offered more opportunities for the managers to collaborate and communicate their differing perspectives.

This dialogue uncovered some company-wide problems, such as the continued need for transparency across divisions, the demand for consistent problem solving among managers, and the fact that IBM product groups were overstretched. In response to issues, the company created the Cross-Team Workouts. These "workouts" were weekly meetings between sales and delivery teams and were designed to provide much-needed transparency, offer an exchange of ideas, and even develop online training in the company's intranet to walk managers through solutions to common conflicts.

IBM understood conflict as a normal part of life, and instead of avoiding its presence, the organization developed a system to boost communication and collaboration—certainly a driver in the company's global success.

GREAT TAKEAWAYS

Remember, with so many personalities working under the same roof, conflict is inevitable. How that conflict is managed will ultimately determine whether the team thrives or fails. Dysfunction can infect an organization if it is not handled properly. The key is to find a way to solve the conflict and get everyone back on the same page. Understanding the different roles individuals take in a conflict is a crucial part of defusing a bad situation.

The Chicago Bears and the Los Angeles Lakers refused to play the role of the victim. The Bears players didn't give up their season due to conflict, and the Lakers management didn't allow the Kobe-Shaq feud to derail the team's three finals appearances. Further, both teams were proactive about solving the conflict. The Bears players made a conscious decision to remove themselves from the standoff between Mike Ditka and Buddy Ryan. The Lakers continued to play team basketball and left Shaquille O'Neal and Kobe Bryant to solve their feud on their own time.

Ideally, though, in the same way that Rick Hendrick stepped in to facilitate understanding between Jimmie Johnson and Chad Knaus, and corporate great IBM enacted a new program for better communication, collaboration is the most successful approach to handling organizational conflict. Teams should create open forums where all parties can discuss and debate their points of view in a respectful manner, and where compromise and resolution are encouraged. Getting all perspectives out in the open can reduce the conflict and keep it from infecting a team from within. As was the case with IBM, this process may even save time and money and prevent future stress by bringing previously undetected problems to light.

If you are currently experiencing conflict with your team, remember the Karpman Drama Triangle of the victim, persecutor, and rescuer. Consider where you might fit in the model and how you can address these issues with your team.

Remember, too, that conflict must be addressed to avoid derailing team goals. Ideally, you and your team can embrace the conflict as a learning opportunity. Seek to understand the reasons behind the conflict and how your team can use conflict as fuel, growing in the process as IBM did. Great Teams don't falter in the face of friction but grow stronger when addressing it directly.

CHAPTER 8

GREAT TEAMS BUILD A MENTORING CULTURE

They encourage everyone to teach and learn every day.

The most successful and high-performing teams strategically embed professional guidance within their cultures to inspire teaching and learning at every opportunity. Mentoring requires a large time commitment and is often neglected in organizations that fail to grasp its value and don't understand how it works. (It's more than a mandatory check-in over coffee.) But Great Teams understand how powerful the synergy can be between veterans and recruits, especially when both mentors and mentees have clearly defined responsibilities to make the relationship successful. Strong mentors embody the tradition, wisdom, and accountability needed to establish and reinforce great culture; these are the leaders who inspire others to improve.

Ultimately, a strong mentoring culture unlocks consistent winning and corporate advancement.

GREAT TEAMS IN SPORTS

In any sport, two of a coach's most important responsibilities are fostering learning and developing talent. For Bob Bowman, head swimming coach of Arizona State University, a dedication to that duty has created one of the greatest Olympians of all time—Michael Phelps.

Phelps, who dominated the Beijing and London Olympic Games, is one of the most decorated athletes in any sport, yet his accomplishments were made possible by the persistent coaching of Bowman, his strategist and mentor.

The two met at the North Baltimore Aquatic Club when Phelps was ten years old. Initially they avoided one another—Phelps didn't like Bowman's authoritative style, and Bowman didn't want to babysit Phelps. But they eventually put aside their differences and became one of the most successful mentor-mentee duos of all time, thanks to Phelps's exceptional talent and Bowman's eye for potential.

Bowman instilled self-belief in Phelps through a grueling yet successful training model that centered on consistent pressure, everyday excellence, and plain old hard work. Bowman told Phelps, often irately, not to rely on his dominating physical body, which was uniquely crafted for swimming. If he wanted to become a world champion, he needed to persistently train harder than anyone else. Bowman's insistence on mental toughness and commitment ignited a fire in the young Phelps. He became obsessed with becoming the best in the world and often went years without missing a single practice.

And the dedication has paid off. Phelps is the holder of dozens of world records, including the most Olympic gold medals (eighteen), the most gold-medal finishes at a single Olympic Games (eight, at the 2008 Games in Beijing), and the most Olympic medals of all time (twenty-two total medals).

"I think that self-belief is very important in a great athlete," Bowman said in a video created by Octagon Speakers Group. "Because ultimately, at the critical moment, they're going to have to rely on the things they have learned, the training that they have done, and pull that all together with their self-concept. That's going to be the most important thing when they go into competition."[1]

Phelps's relationship with Bowman has been so beneficial that he has followed his mentor to head coaching tenures across the country in order to continue his training. And Bowman's life has been equally affected by Phelps and his dedication to win. After serving as assistant coach to three Olympic teams, Bowman was appointed head coach of the US swim team for the 2016 Olympics.[2] But his mentor relationship with Phelps remained a top priority.

"As long as he's swimming, I'm going to coach him," Bowman said in an interview with the *Baltimore Sun*. "He's done so much for me, and that's my commitment to him."[3]

Though a formal arrangement between two people of different ranks is the best-known type of mentoring, a peer-to-peer relationship can have quite a strong influence too. Seasoned leaders of an organization can greatly influence new hires because they work shoulder to shoulder with them every day. In fact, NFL teams drafting young quarterbacks will often keep an older quarterback on the roster as a mentor. This practice shortcuts the trial-and-error process and gives the young player a larger perspective from someone who has already been there.

Such practices are not without drawbacks, of course, especially in the highly competitive world of sports. Many veteran players have a hard time being mentors to younger players who, presumably, will take the veterans' jobs one day; the very idea is counterintuitive. But proper mentoring can still be fostered in the right situations. The challenge for leaders is to clearly define each role and especially to establish a team-first culture in which individual players support each other for the good of the team.

In 2001, twenty-six-year-old quarterback Matt Hasselbeck had just been traded from the Green Bay Packers and was beginning his first year with the Seattle Seahawks. The Seahawks expected Hasselbeck to become a standout starter for his new team.

But it wouldn't be easy. Veteran quarterback Trent Dilfer, fresh from winning a Super Bowl with the Baltimore Ravens, had also been signed by the Seahawks that year. His role was made clear from the beginning—to guide Hasselbeck and serve as an insurance plan should the younger man not perform well. Dilfer did both glowingly, not only filling in for Hasselbeck in big games due to injury but also providing frequent advice to the young quarterback.

When injuries plagued Dilfer's 2002 season, thirty-five-year-old veteran quarterback Jeff George joined Seattle to serve as an emergency backup. But he also became a guiding resource for Hasselbeck. One day during warm-ups before a game in Seattle, Hasselbeck was on the field when a fan started yelling his name. He eventually waved to acknowledge the fan, but it wasn't enough; the fan beckoned Hasselbeck to come over to autograph an item. When Hasselbeck politely declined, the fan became abusive and heckled him.

George noticed that Hasselbeck was bothered by the heckling and stepped in to give the young player some sage advice: "If that kind of stuff is going to bother you, you probably should get out of the business."

"Jeff was absolutely right," Hasselbeck recalled later. "You can't let things like that get under your skin."

The influence of Dilfer and George was pivotal for young Hasselbeck. They helped shape him into the dynamic player he would grow to be—ultimately leading the Seahawks to the Super Bowl in 2006. Their relationships also demonstrate the strong mentoring culture at work with the Seahawks. Such a culture is enormously beneficial for both teams and players.

Jeff Van Gundy, ESPN analyst and former head coach for the New York Knicks and Houston Rockets, has developed some of the most dynamic NBA players in the league and, thanks to his experiences, has come up with what he calls the "two knucklehead theory." Van Gundy's premise is that a professional team will almost always have at least one knucklehead in the group—someone who naturally ruffles everyone else's feathers.

According to Van Gundy, you can have *one* knucklehead, but you can't have two. Two knuckleheads will battle one another or, worse, combine forces and create a bigger problem for the team. When you have only one knucklehead, that guy can't go anywhere to throw his tantrums. Eventually he'll have to fall in line with the makeup of the roster.

No one has seen Van Gundy's theory at work more than Steve Kerr, head coach of the Golden State Warriors. Not only did Kerr lead the team to the NBA title in 2015, his first year as a head coach, but before that he also had the unique experience of playing for the championship-winning Chicago Bulls and San Antonio Spurs under head coaches Phil Jackson and Gregg Popovich, respectively. Under their leadership, he closely observed how mentoring could transform abrasive athletes into high performers and team players.

"I think the brilliance of Pop and Phil was that they embraced the one knucklehead," said Kerr. "In Chicago, when Dennis Rodman came to our team, Phil spoke with him about Native American tribes and how they utilized eccentric personalities in order to add value to their community. In a sense, Phil told Rodman that the team needed the edge and difference that he brought."

The Spurs provide an amazing study on the concept of player-to-player mentoring. Spurs team leader Tim Duncan often volunteers to help with other players so that Coach Popovich's leadership and voice "would not become old," according to Kerr.

"That kind of fair representation of mentors stepping in to manage the moment just makes the coach's job that much easier," Kerr said. "For players, sometimes it is hard to answer to the same authority every single day. When direction comes from a teammate instead, you hear a different voice, and it carries a little more weight after a while."

Mentorship within the ranks of the Spurs did not start with Duncan, however. The success of this five-time NBA champion team—one of the most consistent franchises in the league—is partly due to a tradition of mentorship. It can be clearly seen in the 1997–98 season, Popovich's second year as head coach, when the organization drafted Duncan with the number-one overall pick.

Though Duncan would eventually be the catalyst of Popovich's teams, he entered the NBA as a talented yet unproven rookie. Popovich paired Duncan with center David Robinson—also a former number-one overall pick and the elder statesman of the team—in order to set him up for success. Robinson and Duncan quickly became friends, even though it was clear that Duncan was about to become the face of the franchise, displacing Robinson. Instead of allowing ego to detract from Duncan's potential, Robinson gladly accepted his role as the younger player's mentor.

But Robinson, too, had benefited from team mentorship—from Popovich himself. Robinson had attended the United States Naval Academy and had even skipped the first two years of his NBA career to fulfill his service obligation after graduating. During that time, Popovich was the scout in charge of watching Robinson, who was playing on the Armed Forces basketball team to keep in shape.

Coach Popovich would go see Robinson play, and the two would often go to dinner afterward to get to know each other. Popovich also had a military background, having served five years of active duty in the Air Force, so the two understood each other. The respect between them was always strong, and Popovich's mentorship made Robinson feel he had an important role on the team. So when Duncan showed up, Robinson paid his new teammate the same type of respect that Popovich had once shown him.

"When Tim came, the very first thing I told him was, 'I'm going to put you in position where you can succeed. Period. That's it. If you're a better scorer than me, I'll put you down on the block, you score. I don't care. I can do other things,'" Robinson told ESPN in 2012. "I think [the attitude] permeates a whole franchise. It wasn't me necessarily bringing it in. Popovich is always talking about team. He leads it by saying, 'I don't want any attention. I'm not going to act like I want attention.'"[4]

As years passed, Duncan transitioned into Robinson's role, and by 2001 he had established himself as one of the most selfless, straight-edged superstars in the NBA. That season the Spurs had a young player by the name of Stephen Jackson, who, in his second year, had already developed a reputation as a hothead. Jackson would frequently lash out with profanities at coaches, teammates, opponents, referees, and some-times fans.

Duncan recognized both Jackson's potential and his possible pit-falls and took it upon himself to take the young player under his wing, joking with him and using every opportunity to show the young player how to act like a professional. On more than one occasion, Duncan told Popovich, "I got him." Then he'd go sit with Jackson.

And Duncan didn't stop with Jackson. His calm leadership con-tinues to have an impact on the Spurs. During the team's 2014 NBA championship—its fifth title since 1999—quiet stars like Kawhi Leonard and Danny Green were praised by the future Hall of Fame player in such a way that they elevated their performances to championship heights. Their success, in large part, is due to his leadership through example and intentional motivation.

The established mentorship culture within the Spurs extends off the court as well. Many of today's front-office executives and head coaches around the league attribute at least part of their career success to their early days with the Spurs organization, which equipped them with the tools to rise through the ranks. Because of this type of leadership, the Spurs have earned the reputation as a model franchise.

"To have sustained excellence over a decade is extremely difficult, and the Spurs have done it as well as anyone. What is really impressive is their player development, the fact that they've brought in so many inter-national players and integrated them into a system," football front-office executive Scott Pioli said, observing the application of such powerful les-sons across any sport or organization.[5]

AND FOR THE TRULY GREAT TEAMS IN BUSINESS

Regardless of whether you are a student in higher education, an entry-level employee, or a seasoned professional, finding a mentor to guide your path is the hallmark of a successful career. Like the most successful teams in sports, many of the high-performing organizations in business make mentoring a priority. In a recent study, the American Society for Training and Development reported that 71 percent of Fortune 500 companies surveyed offered a corporate mentorship program to build and equip tomorrow's leaders. The ASTD researchers also discovered that 75 percent of corporate executives credit their rise in leadership directly to their relationships with mentors.[6]

Commander Rorke Denver, speaker, author, actor, and former Navy SEAL, believes that mentorship is a "countercultural act" that defies the self-preservation instinct across business and leadership. Denver's military experience hinged on mentorship and not only made the difference between success and failure but also life and death.

"In the SEAL teams we figured out very, very early on that specific mentorship of connecting a senior officer to a junior officer has a tremendous value," Denver said. "It's a fundamental thing that SEAL development looks at. The minute you stop learning and stop seeking out growth opportunities, you'll begin to rot pretty quickly."

Denver is correct. Leaders owe it to themselves and their organizations to shape new talent or else they are setting their teams up for failure.

The American multinational corporation General Electric has a strong foundation of growing leaders through mentorship. College graduates hired into General Electric immediately join the Experienced Commercial Leadership Program (ECLP), described by the company as "the premier development opportunity for GE's future sales and marketing leaders."[7] Training within the ECLP consists of three extensive assignments over two years as part of the marketing and sales areas of GE's businesses, where employees learn best practices from corporate veterans and ultimately enhance their own leadership skills. Employees who excel in the ECLP usually find themselves on a managerial track in one of General Electric's branches—GE Energy Connections, GE Power,

GE Healthcare, GE Capital, GE Aviation, GE Lighting, GE Oil and Gas, GE Transportation, and GE Global Growth & Operations—where they are well positioned for growth within the corporation.[8]

Technology manufacturer Intel, inventor of the modern micro-processor and one of the world's largest semiconductor-chip makers, has taken a very different route to developing its talent. Instead of matching fresh recruits with veterans, as most organizations do, Intel has created a process that connects individuals on the basis of high-demand skills. The mentees—whom Intel calls "partners"—choose topics that interest them, and an Intel questionnaire and extensive employee database match the recruits with mentors who are subject-matter experts in those areas.

Intel has three rules for its mentoring relationships: 1) partners govern the relationship, create meeting dates, and ultimately decide what they would like to work on; 2) mentors and partners draw up a contract that contains the details of the mentoring relationship; and 3) terms and limitations are left to be discussed and decided upon by the mentor and partner, *not* Intel.[9]

The fact that employees can access Intel's innovative mentoring system through e-mail and company intranet expands the mentoring reach across the company's international employee pool. The result is a diverse, open stream of information sharing that ultimately fuels growth by shaping the company culture.

The success of corporate mentorship programs developed by some of the Great Teams in business demonstrates how powerful this concept can be and what a difference it can make. As Intel and General Electric have shown, when a corporate culture includes mentorship, the end result is a dynamic learning environment with leaders constantly shaping leaders.

GREAT TAKEAWAYS

A mentoring culture is as important to a company as its road map. No matter what business you are in, having willing mentors throughout your organization will help build and sustain greatness in the long run.

Here are several steps leaders can take to create an effective, high-performing culture of mentorship.

1. Be intentional about setting up mentoring relationships. This may mean setting up a formal program or simply matching up recruits with veterans or professionals with similar skill sets.

2. Train employees at all levels to recognize every moment as a mentoring moment.

3. Encourage team members at all levels to ask for mentoring opportunities. Many mentoring relationships never begin because no one is willing to risk rejection. If possible, management should initiate by extending those invitations to its talent.

4. Foster a team-first mentality throughout the company, and engage team members at all levels with the purpose of their work. Workers who are focused on helping the team reach its goals will be more likely to make the sacrifices necessary to bring everyone up to speed.

5. Remember that "team first" applies to everyone— including the mentors. Avoid penalizing them by making a mentorship just another assigned task piled up on top of all the others. Build in time for mentorship and try to offer other benefits beyond good feelings.

6. Combat jealousy and fear of mentoring by making roles and outcomes clear at the outset. Avoid the kind of "I trained them, but now they've taken my job" scenarios that team members may rightly fear.

7. Remind everyone that what goes around comes around. Leaders should remember their beginnings, not just their current positions of prominence. Then they must reciprocate the help they received along the way by reaching out to the next wave of leaders.

In our fast-paced world, every organization desires an edge over competitors. As the Great Teams profiled in this chapter demonstrate, making mentoring part of a team culture is a great way to provide that edge.

Everyone benefits when an organization places high value on developing young employees. Mentees, of course, are given a leg up as mentoring relationships accelerate upward mobility. Mentors gain something from these relationships too—such as receiving a differing perspective about a common area of interest. But the biggest benefit of all is to the team as a whole. Ultimately, mentoring relationships help retain employees, create a brimming pool of talent uniquely molded to fit into company culture, increase the quality of leadership, and provide the growth to set a great organization apart from its competitors.

It's one of those factors that ultimately makes a good team great.

CHAPTER 9

GREAT TEAMS ADJUST QUICKLY TO LEADERSHIP TRANSITIONS

They endure change and keep their established cultures intact.

In sports and business, transition is inevitable. Acquisitions, mergers, promotions, demotions, and organizational shuffles are common in both worlds, and the day-to-day adjustment to those transitions often happens at a high level. Any organization will be uniquely challenged when responding to employee retirement, resignation, or termination—but Great Teams adjust more quickly than their opponents and do not allow leadership change to derail their missions. Instead of losing momentum and letting change becoming an excuse for failure, the leaders of these organizations allow moments of change to accelerate their teams' success.

GREAT TEAMS IN SPORTS

In the sports world, changes of leadership can happen at the drop of a hat. Injury or physical decline can put star players out of commission suddenly, or they may simply decide to retire. Personality or ego clashes between key personnel can lead to the ouster of one or another—as in the Kobe Bryant–Shaquille O'Neal conflict profiled in chapter 7. And the pressure of winning often forces teams to change coaches or managers. Just ask the NFL's Oakland Raiders, who have gone through *nine* head coaches since 2002. Sadly for Raiders fans, these personnel shuffles haven't helped develop a competitive team.

In truth, such serial changes in leadership are usually a temporary solution to a cultural problem. The well-being of an organization requires order and vision, not musical-chairs leadership. In fact, a high turnover rate among the leadership can cripple an organization—but not always.

In 1978, for instance, the New York Yankees went through three managers—Billy Martin, Dick Howser, and Bob Lemon—and still had one hundred victories in the regular season, mowed through the competition in the playoffs, and won the World Series. Three years later, in 1981, the Yankees did it again. They went through two managers and still made it back to the World Series.

And the Washington Redskins, under Coach Joe Gibbs, managed to make four Super Bowl appearances and win three titles in the 1980s and early 1990s—while playing a game of musical quarterbacks. Each title game featured a different QB: Joe Theismann in 1982, Doug Williams in 1987, and Mark Rypien in 1991.

"It was amazing because the goal is just the opposite," former Washington offensive line coach Joe Bugel remembered later. "Every team is looking for that franchise quarterback who the rest of the team can rally around. With Joe Gibbs, we just executed and executed. We could change running backs, wide receivers, tight ends, even the quarterback. The only thing we didn't change much was the offensive line. We were lucky there."

Doug Williams further elaborated that Gibbs focused on preparation: "We were totally confident when we played. You knew exactly what you were supposed to do, and you knew exactly what the guy next to you was supposed to do." He added, "We were all on the same page all the time. If a player changed, no problem. Next man up."

Great Teams, in other words, respond to a change of leadership by stepping up to the plate. They are able to focus on the task ahead and keep moving because players and personnel understand that the coach, the manager, or the quarterback is not the centerpiece of the team.

Life is change, and organizations that understand how to handle transitions in leadership are always the most successful. As discussed in earlier chapters, this is built by creating depth to handle such situations and developing a team culture based on shared values, principles, and purpose. A team that has internalized such a culture will have the resilience to weather leadership transitions without veering off course.

One of the greatest leadership transitions in sports history began with a tragedy. In 1993 the Chicago Bulls were on top of the world. Led by NBA superstars Michael Jordan and Scottie Pippen, both in the prime of their careers, the Bulls were only the third team in NBA history to "three-peat" as champions.

But the celebration ended when Jordan received news that his father, James R. Jordan Sr., had been murdered in North Carolina. In the wake of his father's death, Jordan decided to walk away from the NBA to pursue his dream of playing professional baseball. The news shook the franchise, Jordan's Bulls teammates, and the NBA as a whole.

Scottie Pippen realized the Bulls needed a new leader, so he stepped up. "It was pretty shocking, and looking back at it, it was emotional too," he said in an interview with NBA.com. "It took us all by surprise, but it didn't change anything in terms of what we had to do as players. We had to focus on preparing for another season. We had to stick to our routines, continue to train, and be ready for camp. Michael retiring opened up an opportunity for us to show that we were still a very good team."[1]

To compensate for losing Jordan, the Bulls added key players Toni Kukoč, Bill Wennington, Steve Kerr, and Luc Longley—all of whom would become pivotal in the future of the franchise. Under Coach Phil Jackson, the Bulls remained successful over the next two years with Pippen as the face of the team, making it to the Eastern Conference semifinals both seasons. During that span, Pippen shaped his own all-star resume and cemented his place as one of the best in the league.

"Scottie moved into that [leadership] position with a tremendous amount of comfort," Jackson said in a 2010 NBA.com interview. "He was always a very good person on and off the court. He understood his teammates and he helped them out. That was a major development in Scottie's career."[2]

Toward the end of the 1994–95 season, Jordan once again shocked the sports world with a simple faxed press release that read: "I'm back."[3]

The announcement solidified Jordan's choice to abandon his baseball career and rejoin the Bulls. He even accepted less money to make sure he could come back. Though the undisputed leader of the team, Pippen understood the situation and humbly stepped aside to relinquish the leadership role back to Jordan.

Jordan appeared at the most opportune moment. With seventeen games left in the 1994–1995 season, the Bulls were a ho-hum 34–31 and in danger of missing the playoffs. In his first game after nearly two years away, Jordan scored nineteen points; in his fourth game, he hit a game-winning jump shot at the buzzer. Then, in the fifth game he scored fifty-five points at Madison Square Garden against the New York Knicks. Jordan's comeback was a show of strength that made it clear that his rust was only minimal and that he would soon get back to being the league's most dominant force.

Jordan helped Chicago to a 13–4 record to close the season, although Pippen still led the team in every major statistical category—including a great attitude.

"Scottie was definitely one of the reasons I came back," Jordan told the *Chicago Tribune* in 1997. "I sat in the locker room [the season after Jordan retired] and asked him how it was, how he felt, and he was suffering. He was taking the brunt of the rebuilding process and he shouldn't have been. I could feel he wanted me back basketball-wise, and as a friend. And I missed him too."[4]

Jordan also returned with a better appreciation of Pippen. "I know he makes me a better player," he said. "Unfortunately, it may take a while, after we both retire, for people to realize just how good Scottie Pippen really was."[5]

After Jordan's return, the Bulls went on to win another three championships in a row—including an eye-popping seventy-two-win season—solidifying its legacy as one of the most prolific dynasties in NBA history.

AND FOR THE TRULY GREAT TEAMS IN BUSINESS

Today's corporate world runs at warp speed, and change is a given. In order to compete in this fluid landscape, leaders must embrace change as an asset and not something to be feared.

Great Teams understand change well enough to navigate it to success. They use transition as an opportunity to gain an edge over the competition. But since most people are creatures of habit and suspicious of change—especially in the workplace—leading a transition is not easy.

The grooming model and the gap model for leadership transitions are often used by corporations to handle these situations with poise.

The grooming model may work best for organizations expecting a change in leadership in the coming months or years—typically with a retirement on the horizon or a shift in executive leadership. It tends to be most successful when a team has been consistently successful and stable and the outgoing manager is a Relational, Expert, or Charismatic leader (as discussed in chapter 2).

Using this model, the outgoing leader typically has a significant amount of input in choosing a successor and transferring knowledge to that successor at a strategic pace. Additionally, this incumbent can oversee the transition and learn from the process. In the event that a successor can't be found, the grooming model offers enough time for a backup plan to be developed.

The grooming model sounds ideal, but a transition dilemma can occur if there is confusion in the ranks about whose leadership to follow—the outgoing leader or the successor. Also, the search for not just any successor, but the *right* successor, can prove extremely time consuming and expensive. According to research at the Florida State University College of Business, in 2012, there were ninety-four situations where public companies issued a press release that a successor had been identified, but only 38 percent of these candidates actually took the posts they were recruited to fill. This can happen when an outgoing leader resists relinquishing control to a successor, thus becoming reengaged with the professional team, developing a faction, and eliminating the successor altogether.

An incoming leader can manage such a challenge by learning the outgoing manager's leadership style. Successors should try to maintain as much communication with the outgoing leader as possible and also build a balanced network of connections with people who both liked and disliked the outgoing leader. Doing so can dissolve a faction.

The gap model, on the other hand, consists of phasing out old leadership, planning a transitioning stage between the older leader's last day and the successor's first day, and then phasing in the new leader. With this model, team members have a bigger say in choosing the successor, changes are made with fewer political implications, and the transition is easier for an incoming leader and the team. Organizations should use the gap model when the outgoing leader is a Command and Control leader who seeks to maintain control when the team needs a complete turnaround.

There can be variations within these two models, of course. One version of the grooming model would involve a very powerful Command and Control handpicking a successor and then attempting to control the company *through* the successor. Or in the case of a leader who drops down suddenly without a plan in place, a company would have to use a modified gap model to phase in a successor as soon as possible—or perhaps appoint an interim leader until a new permanent one can be selected.

Regardless of the transition method used, new leaders will always be faced with the challenge of keeping the organization running while getting up to speed. This is true when everything is going well but especially relevant when there are difficulties—financial struggles, legal questions, or simply dwindling morale or confusion in the workforce.

Sharon Price John, CEO and "Chief President Bear" of Build-A-Bear Workshop—where shoppers can make and customize their very own stuffed animals—returned her organization to profitability after she joined the company in 2013. Build-A-Bear had just recorded a six-month loss in profits, so company and employee morale were at an all-time low. John realized her strategic plan could not simply be a list of objectives. She needed to be an energetic, actionable visionary who evolved her organization and ensured the well-being of her employees.

John and her executive team intelligently communicated their vision to elicit buy-in from the rest of the company, but for employees the transition proved difficult. To combat doubt, naysaying, and dismay as the difficulties mounted, John executed an extensive internal marketing campaign to remind employees of the vision.

One of their most successful tactics was orchestrating "disruptive moments"—breaks in the daily corporate routine intended to make workers smile and keep them interested, engaged, and committed to the company's mission. This included corny slogans such as "Bear-lieve" and "Drive to the Dollar"—the campaign cry intended to help employees remember the company's six-month profitability goal. "Drive to the Dollar" became a company-wide screen saver—a hard to ignore memory aid—and employees could e-mail ideas on how to improve efficiency to an official "Drive to the Dollar" account.

With the company empowered by the messaging and vision, attitudes and habits began to shift. By the end of 2013—and for the first time in years—the organization returned to profitability. And none of that would have happened if not for John and her executive team's plan for handling the human response to transition.

Build-A-Bear's management identified five behavior-based actions that they, as leaders, could do to ease the discomfort of a change:

1. Be visibly passionate about the vision; keep frustrations private.
2. Reiterate the long-term vision and specific goals as often as possible.
3. Monitor the corporate mind-set regularly and informally. Ask questions and listen. "Management by walking around" (MBWA) is an excellent way to do this.
4. Identify progress and negativity quickly. Reward progress and make changes where negativity persists.
5. Frequently remind the organization that it is being asked to act differently in order to achieve different results.[6]

"Change is almost always uncomfortable and exhausting," John wrote in a 2014 op-ed for *Fortune* magazine. "You are asking your organization to do something in a new way—every day—until it's a habit. The 'old' habits may have taken years to form and were likely linked to rewards, so it's normal for individuals and teams to revert to what's comfortable when difficulties or confusions arise."[7]

Recent business history has seen a flurry of acquisitions and mergers, including some landmark ones—Disney and Pixar, Sirius and XM radio, Exxon and Mobil. Many of these transitions have gone quite well. But even in the best scenarios, such massive change in an organization can be problematic. Problems can develop from the sudden increase in employees, teams, and leaders, all of whom have to be unified under a new banner of leadership and culture.

Jennifer Reimert, former vice president of software giant Symantec, knows this better than anyone. In 2005, Symantec acquired Veritas Software in order to gain a competitive edge; however, the move more than doubled Symantec's staff—to fourteen thousand—and created engagement problems with far-flung employees. Communication suffered, cooperation dwindled, and disengagement grew. Silicon Valley watchdogs, keenly observing the merger, even recruited and hired away Symantec employees.

"Leadership through a transition is crucial, but often we forget to focus on developing one culture out of two," Reimert said. "Symantec bought something bigger than itself when we acquired Veritas. When that happens, managers must ask themselves, 'What happens to leadership? Where do I go now? This team doesn't know me, how can I improve that?'"

Reimert and her team sought to correct these failures with a more effective way to reward outstanding members of their huge employee base for good service. Later that year, the company introduced Applause, an employee recognition program that rewarded high performers. Applause not only recognized the top 15 percent of the company's employees, but also served as a driver for refreshing Symantec's corporate culture and reinforcing the company's values of innovation, trust, and customer-driven action. As Reimert put it, "Applause brought our two companies together, rebuilt trust among our old and new employee base, repurposed our values, and informed everyone of what it means to work at Symantec."

With Applause, Symantec placed the power of recognition at the ground level. Employees were empowered to congratulate and celebrate the accomplishments of colleagues who did outstanding work or provided innovative ideas. And staff members could suggest handsome compensation to coworkers for a job well done—the rewards ranged from twenty-five to a thousand dollars.

Employee response to Applause was overwhelmingly positive. Job satisfaction and cooperation soared as people rewarded one another enthusiastically. Production rose as employees strove for recognition themselves. And by centralizing the process, Symantec reached more employees than ever and strengthened its corporate culture.

"Adoption spread very quickly," Reimert said. "Once the Applause program began, employees helped carry it out. And once people receive, then they want to give—which spread the program."

Reimert said Applause truly resonates with Symantec employees since it "brought out the good" and "celebrated the contributions of others."

"Every recognition moment is connected back to your values, and we were trying to repurpose our values to carry our company forward," Reimert said. "Leaders have to start rebuilding by identifying what is broken and then rebuilding trust. These connections should have a real meaning to everyone, no matter where they are in the company."

GREAT TAKEAWAYS

The number one cause of breakdown during leadership change is failing to adjust to a new situation effectively. Here are some suggestions for handling leadership transitions—big or small—with a minimum of trauma:

1. Try to have a transition plan in place before it becomes necessary. Leadership changes are unavoidable, and it's only wise to prepare in advance.
2. Carefully determine the transition model that will work best for the organization. This could be a grooming model, a gap model, or a variation of either.
3. Outgoing leaders can lessen the difficulty of a leadership phase-out by setting strict departure dates, building a transition plan (if one is not already in place), and constructing a best-practices document for their successors.
4. If appropriate, select an interim leader and set up operating procedures to keep the organization moving forward as the organization shifts.
5. Search teams or recruiters should strive for transparency and open communication in the process of finding new leaders. This doesn't mean everyone has to weigh in on the decision, but those whose lives will be affected by a change deserve to be kept informed.

6. Clearly communicate the end goal of the transition and the new leader's agenda to everyone involved—from top leadership to rank-and-file employees.

7. Always remember the importance of employee buy-in for a new leadership regime. Employ creative strategies to build goodwill within the organization.

In sports or in business, leadership changes don't have to spell disaster. Any organization can emerge from a transition stronger and better equipped for the future if it approaches the process strategically, maintains a strong team culture, and focuses on the greater purpose to minimize disruptions and propel the organization forward toward a bright new future.

CHAPTER 10

GREAT TEAMS ADAPT AND EMBRACE CHANGE

They understand that past results might not guarantee future success.

Charles Darwin has been quoted as saying, "It is not the strongest or the most intelligent who will survive, but those who can best manage change."[1] And as we've seen in the previous chapter, the sports and business landscapes are constantly transitioning both internally and externally. What sowed success one year might not necessarily work the next.

Being resistant—or even oblivious—to change is a common mistake. Great Teams keep their eyes open to what is going on and tweak their methods to ensure an ability to thrive in changing circumstances. At the same time, their leaders remain mentally tough and understand the importance of focusing on the task at hand in the midst of changing circumstances.

In this chapter, we will look at how great winners welcome new ideas and strategies to consistently return to championship heights.

GREAT TEAMS IN SPORTS

NCAA men's basketball offers special case studies in adaptation, since the new normal consists of coaching one-and-done athletes who go pro after just one year of collegiate play. For Mike Krzyzewski of Duke and John Calipari of the University of Kentucky—head coaches to two of the most consistently successful basketball programs in the country—mastering change requires teaching new generations differently while maintaining core values.

"Our culture is still value based," Krzyzewski said, who had three freshmen declare for the NBA Draft after winning the 2015 NCAA championship. "Trust, honesty, teamwork, loyalty, care, and collective responsibility—all of these things are the same over my three decades at Duke, but they are taught differently than twenty years ago, because communication changes as well."

Adjustment, especially in communication methods, is constant for Krzyzewski in order to remain relevant and at the top of his profession. He says Duke's values are "taught differently and by different people" today than they were when he won his first title in 1988—before any of his current players were even born!

"The younger players see the world differently," Krzyzewski said. "And it's up to you as the communicator to know who you are addressing. It is not some sort of science, but more about knowing people and wanting to learn more about them and not making those athletes fit into a thing that you did a year ago. Adjustment is hard, but is a lot easier if you, as a leader, are a willing learner."

Likewise, John Calipari has maintained a winning culture that regularly recruits the one-and-done players who are attracted to Kentucky for the sole reason of wanting to increase their odds of playing in the NBA. And he does it by relying on team culture and values for stability in the midst of change. "The core values go through everything we do," Calipari said. "Our style of play changes every year because, more than any other program in the history of college basketball, we have turnover. But if you stick with your core values, your teams year in and year out will look the same."

Kentucky's core values are servant leadership, family, and trust—all characteristics that Calipari imparts during recruitment. "When we recruit, we don't oversell and underdeliver, we undersell and overdeliver," he said. "And when we abide by our core values and make it about players, building them as student athletes so they can withstand the ups and downs of life in basketball, then we are successful."

Beach volleyball champions Misty May-Treanor and Kerri Walsh Jennings are shining examples of athletes who have mastered the art of adjusting to change. Over the span of eight years—starting with their first tour championship in 2001 and ending with their second gold medal in the 2008 Olympics—they displayed stunning streaks of dominance. In the months leading up to the 2008 Games in Beijing, they didn't lose a single set in any match.

A lot changed after that triumph in Beijing, however. May-Treanor was invited to compete on ABC's *Dancing With the Stars* program in the fall of 2008, but she ruptured her Achilles tendon while practicing. That's potentially a career-ending injury for an athlete whose sport depends on explosive jumping. The subsequent surgery and extensive rehab side-lined May-Treanor.

Meanwhile, Walsh Jennings faced her own physical challenges with the births of her first two children in 2009 and 2010. She sat out both years to be with her growing family.

By 2011, when the two decided to come back for a third run at a gold medal, many things had changed. Aside from surgery and child-birth, both athletes were now in their thirties. They were different people now, both physically and mentally, and they struggled to get into sync. During a run of eleven international tournaments in 2011, the duo won only three games.

The start of the 2012 season was worse; May-Treanor and Walsh Jennings lost five tournaments and finished higher than fifth only once. By that point, the team was dealing with the ultimate killer for athletes: a serious lack of confidence.

"We were trying to find this easy answer—should we jump higher or move faster?—but we discovered that it was never physical," Walsh Jennings said. "It was only mental and emotional."

At Walsh Jennings's request, the pair visited a sports psychologist she had been seeing since 2009. Although May-Treanor didn't necessarily see the value in the counseling at first, she strongly believed it was the best thing to do for the team.

"Our time in sports psychology was pretty much about seeing what we wanted and doing everything we could to make that happen," May-Treanor said. "But it was also about, how do we get balanced? What I mean by that is Kerri sometimes gets really amped up. So . . . what does she need to focus on to bring her down so that we perform at a certain level? What fires me up to get to performance level, and how do I maintain it?"

It was important for the team to adjust their mental game so that they could continue to have chemistry, even if they were not in peak physical condition as before. Working with the sports psychologist forced both players to look at how they worked together; May-Treanor tended to be more laid back in her approach, and Walsh Jennings was more anxious, particularly when the team struggled. Instead of letting those qualities grate on each other as the team tried to find its way, they learned how to play off each other's mental cues.

In the 2012 Olympics in London, the pair was seeded number three, but every team still desired to beat them on the international stage. "Obviously we were an underdog, but I don't think we looked at ourselves as one," May-Treanor said. "We looked back and thought of ourselves as champions from 2008. People wanted to beat us, and no matter what we did that season, every time a team stepped on the court against us, people wanted to take us down. Our coach reminded us every day: 'People are there to watch us and want to take us down.' That is a sense of pride, and even though we were seeded third, it didn't matter. There is only going to be one winner. So it doesn't matter what your seed is."

Walsh Jennings and May-Treanor went on to have a career-defining streak at the London Games—thirty-two consecutive sets, all without a loss. Eventually, the duo defeated fellow Americans Jen Kessy and April Ross to win the gold medal once again. Their victory sent a powerful message to the sports world that the greatest winners aren't defined by age or circumstance but by mental toughness and willingness to embrace change in order to be successful.

AND FOR THE TRULY GREAT TEAMS IN BUSINESS

Bill McDermott of SAP said, "Always be who you said you would be to your customer and do things for them that others perhaps wouldn't do." The ability to adapt style of play to current conditions is crucial in business, particularly in a digital world where consumer demands change quickly.

A compelling example of this dynamic comes from the restaurant industry, which is notorious for change but has experienced even bigger shifts in recent years. With start-up costs and risk of failure higher than ever, the food-truck business has literally taken off across the country. Critically dependent on maintaining a customer base, these mobile eateries use Twitter, Facebook, and Instagram to help regular customers find them around town. Just as the food truck itself is an adaptation, so are the business methods that keep it successful.

History contains example after example of organizations that have failed to adapt to change. In the 2000s, America's favorite video titan, Blockbuster, lost its six-billion dollar domination of the home movie rental industry because it ignored rapidly changing consumer trends and technological innovations. Netflix first emerged during this time as a relatively new and unknown organization, but with a superb business model—using inexpensive rentals and convenience to cater to consumers, first with "DVD by mail" and later with video streaming.

Blockbuster did not take the time to research the market and the technological curve that Netflix had founded its business on. Had it done so, the rental giant might have purchased Netflix outright and held onto its lead in the field. Eventually Blockbuster did release and promote a digital version, but Netflix had already beaten them in capturing the online streaming marketplace—solidifying itself as the new global leader of the industry.

In 2008, Verizon expanded its identity beyond "just a phone company," as Verizon Federal president Susan Zeleniak said in an interview for *Washington Technology*.[2] The company desired a critical place in cybersecurity and information technology solutions, so it acquired cell phone operator Alltel Corporation.

That acquisition made Verizon the largest cell-phone provider in the United States. It also increased Verizon's wireless income by 29.6 percent—though even this tremendous boost represented only 57 percent of the organization's revenue.[3] With the leverage from its acquisition, Verizon invested heavily in the security sector, winning multiple government contracts (the focus of Verizon Federal) and creating a strong niche in additional markets such as wireless integration—the communication of devices without cables.

Currently Verizon is an industry leader in security services management. Zeleniak says this accomplishment has helped transform the image of Verizon to that of a multiservice entity with a variety of security and technology solutions—with the federal government as one of its biggest clients.

"[Network security is] probably our federal customers' No. 1 challenge," Zeleniak said. "We run the world's largest Internet, so we have a lot of practical experience; we know what tools it takes and what kind of capabilities it takes to secure a network."[4]

Great companies build diverse teams reflective of our ever-changing, globalized world. For managers who understand its value, such diversity can be a powerful, game-changing tool. Visionary leader Frances Hesselbein, CEO and president of the Frances Hesselbein Leadership Institute, has used diversity to build and shape an entire generation of female leaders. By understanding the value of our multicultural world,

Hesselbein ascended from part-time volunteer to CEO of one of the biggest organizations in the world, the Girl Scouts of the USA.

Hesselbein's path to CEO began when she was a young mother in her hometown of Johnstown, Pennsylvania, where many of her neighbors were international workers employed by the regional coal mines. Living in a community rich with racial and ethnic diversity exposed Hesselbein to the contributions of others who were different than her, which she later credited as something that "determined the type of leader" she would become.

When Hesselbein joined the Girl Scouts as a part-time troop leader, she immediately noticed that the promotional materials were outdated and lacked racial diversity. "There was an enormous opportunity to move forward with our organization," Hesselbein said. "But it would only happen if we realized not all girls look alike, despite what the brochures showed."

Hesselbein took a professional position in the organization and quickly became a rising star, but even as her time in the corner office grew, she never forgot the organization's diversity problem. In 1976, the Girl Scouts internal hiring committee contacted her to interview for CEO. "I thought I'd never leave Pennsylvania," Hesselbein said. "And I never imagined that I'd one day have the chance to lead the largest organization for girls and women around the world."

During her interview, Hesselbein presented her vision, which she described as "a massive change, like a quiet revolution."

Hesselbein declared the Girl Scouts should update the twelve-year-old resource handbooks to promote math, science, and technology—all emerging opportunities for women—and also to appeal to minorities. She also called for a complete overhaul of corporate executive training to include new management resources and modernized communications. The committee hired her on the spot.

"The entire country was in a period of great, positive change, and the committee bought into my ideas of transforming the organization," Hesselbein said.

When Hesselbein became CEO, she inherited an organization in crisis. The Girl Scouts organization was in danger of becoming obsolete or even ceasing to exist as an independent entity. But the leaders of the group, like any Great Team, saw opportunity in the cultural changes surrounding them. Specifically, American women were redefining their places in the home and corporate America. Hesselbein and the Girl Scouts executives saw an opportunity to reach out and speak to that next generation of female leadership. As Hesselbein said, it was a critical commitment to be a part of "that very bright future."

"The Girl Scouts quickly tripled racially and ethnically by making our message reach all girls," Hesselbein said. "We asked ourselves, 'When women and girls look at us, our board, staff, materials, and handbooks, can they find themselves?' So we made a passionate commitment to make that a reality, and our people were ready for it."

Hesselbein's keen observations and incredible leadership—and her organization's willingness to adapt to a changing society—led to the largest growth in the history of the organization, with a membership of 2.25 million girls and a "workforce" of 780,000 volunteers.[5]

GREAT TAKEAWAYS

Los Angeles Clippers vice president of basketball operations Kevin Eastman once said, "If you fight change, you fight the future. If you fight your future, you fight your success."

No organization can hope to succeed in the long term if it does not adapt. Circumstances, times, and people change, and in order to stay competitive, companies must change as well. Great Teams have superb situational awareness—meaning they understand the factors that truly affect performance—and are open to changing their approaches to remain successful.

The first step in embracing change is recognizing the internal and environmental factors that made you successful in the first place. Understanding how these components have changed over time—as

Netflix and the Girl Scouts of the USA did—will help identify what the company needs to do to stay ahead of the competition.

This is the truest definition of adaptation for Great Teams. Consistent winners adapt their game plans based on the tools currently at their disposal and the circumstances of the present—with an eye on the future. They are always on the lookout for new ways to develop an edge against their competitors. And there are no excuses for not doing this. The world's resources lie within reach of our keyboards. With a simple Internet search, an ambitious team can pick up new approaches and advantages.

Achieving success is an evolving process that becomes more challenging with each passing year. But if an organization can acknowledge the reality that past success does not necessarily predict future success, then change becomes an unlikely ally rather than an adversary.

Along with adaptation, an organization must have mental toughness, especially when facing forces outside of their control. Misty May-Treanor summarized it perfectly in a conversation with me: "When you are on a team, you have to be willing to completely sacrifice for the good of the team. Kerri and I knew that something had to change for us to stay on top. She wanted to engage a mental strength coach. I wasn't big on the idea, but I was big on the team—and the idea of winning. We grew together and became mentally tougher. That's why we won London."

Any team desiring to be great must develop the mental edge required to master change. Ultimately, that's what makes the most innovative and undeniably successful teams great.

CHAPTER 11

GREAT TEAMS RUN SUCCESSFUL HUDDLES

They understand that handling meetings is an important part of achieving greatness.

A common frustration among organizations is company meetings, which can trigger negative emotions throughout the levels of any team. Lateness, inattention, overdrawn objectives, and unclear directives are enough to give even the most seasoned professionals a dislike for meetings. But the Great Teams in sports and business use these gatherings in the conference room and on the field—huddles are meetings too!—to inspire confidence, encourage productivity, and create a competitive advantage. They understand the value of getting together in person or via technology to share opinions, coordinate plans, and solidify team culture.

In this chapter, your team will learn how the Great Teams in sports and business run their huddles in ways that promote efficiency, clarity, and championship results.

GREAT TEAMS IN SPORTS

Making sure team members are fully engaged during a huddle is critical. The University of Michigan men's basketball team found that out the hard way during the 1993 NCAA championship game against the University of North Carolina Tar Heels. The Wolverines were down by two points with nineteen seconds left in the game when the team called a time-out, and the players huddled for a critical game plan adjustment.

This huddle led to one of the greatest—and costliest—blunders in sports history.

Gathering the team close, Michigan head coach Steve Fisher calmly reminded the team that they had no time-outs remaining. But not everyone was listening. Some of the Michigan players—those who were not playing—were not paying attention to the huddle. One player was even looking in the stands and waving to Wolverine fans.

Play resumed, and star forward Chris Webber dribbled the ball up court with plenty of time remaining for the Wolverines to get another shot. However, when Webber stopped dribbling and was momentarily trapped, he called another time-out—despite having just gotten the reminder from Coach Fisher. That rule violation resulted in a technical foul, giving North Carolina the ball and the chance to make two free throws.

The result: that night UNC became national champions.

Ultimately, Webber received the brunt of the blame for the mistake, but the replay shows him picking up his dribble and searching desperately for a way out of the trapping UNC defense. A teammate on the sideline yelled for him to call time-out and, in the heat of the moment, Webber complied. Webber's glare after the technical foul call makes it obvious that his teammate—the same one who had been looking in the stands and missing key information during the previous huddle—had given incorrect and inopportune advice, costing the Wolverines the championship.

The coaching elite of NCAA basketball cite Michigan's example as a danger of not being fully engaged during a huddle. Disengagement doesn't happen by chance, but as a direct *result* of team culture. How the players of a team approach huddles is a direct reflection of how important their culture deems meetings.

The art of a meeting is often about leadership. In the world of sports, this leader normally appears as a captain, coach, or a star player who acts as an authority figure or operates as a medium for the team's internal communication. Such leaders have the ability to control each meeting not just because of position but also because they can identify what needs to be heard, what needs to be said, and the best way to say it. Leaders must ensure that meetings work to the benefit of all involved, that each meeting addresses the important issues and disregards the irrelevant ones. They are the ones responsible for engaging team members.

A prime example of this happened during the New England Patriots' run of three Super Bowl titles over a four-year span between 2001 and 2004. New England head coach Bill Belichick is the face of the franchise, and his knowledge of strategy is considered second to none. But assistant coach and defensive coordinator Romeo Crennel (now defensive coordinator for the Houston Texans) created a highly effective and now often-imitated environment for his defensive players' meetings.

Like most professional teams, Belichick and his executive team made meetings an integral part of their weekly preparation. The coaching staff would meet and develop a plan for the upcoming game by the middle of each Tuesday. After these gatherings, Crennel and other assistants would call smaller meetings with the players to relay the detailed specifics of the week's plan. Crennel made it a practice to let his players speak their minds after receiving the plan. With a defense that featured star veterans such as Tedy Bruschi, Willie McGinest, Ty Law, and Mike Vrabel, the coach wisely solicited the players' input about what could work and what they would be comfortable trying to execute.

"A lot of leaders don't have the self-confidence to allow player input," Bruschi said. "Romeo was excellent at saying to us, 'Okay, here's what the coaches have come up with. What do you guys think?' That didn't mean we always got to do what we thought we should do, but we felt like we had a voice and were respected."

Under head coach Bill Walsh, the San Francisco 49ers placed such importance on the art of the meeting that he had specific rules and procedures regarding how each one should run. Walsh analyzed and even recorded meetings to spot potential lulls and weaknesses in their process. He wanted to make sure his assistant coaches—who would sometimes change from year to year—were teaching his team in a consistent fashion.

Quarterback Joe Montana, who came on board right after Walsh did, shared Walsh's high opinion of meetings. This legendary team leader—who won four Super Bowl championships and is tied for the most titles among all quarterbacks—was known in and around the NFL as "Joe Cool." He had an uncanny knack for seeing all aspects of the game from his position on the field and was seemingly unflappable in the most pressurized situations. And there was a reason for Montana's demeanor: like Walsh, he believed in a very diligent, orderly meeting process as a means of keeping players engaged.

For Montana, the huddle was a sacred place and the ultimate comfort zone. There were rules to be followed when Montana was giving out information for the next play. If those rules weren't adhered to, Montana told his teammates to take the issue somewhere else. The huddle was a place where everyone needed to be engaged and headed in the same direction.

"That's what Bill demanded and that started in minicamps and training camp. We were reindoctrinated every single year about what went on in the huddle," former San Francisco offensive lineman Randy Cross said. "Bill figured that the most important piece of communication you could have at any time during the play was the huddle, and to have the chance to clearly figure out what exactly was going on and what the play was."

Cross explained that there were constant changes to the San Francisco offense in those years. Most were small adjustments that required precise execution during a play—which put a further premium on communication.

"I always assumed most coaches demanded the same kind of meeting and huddle discipline that we got from Walsh," Cross admitted. "When I got into broadcasting, I learned that other football organizations didn't communicate like Walsh did. With our team, he used innumerable things that set us apart."

These innumerable things included bluntly educating new players on the disciplined approach to the huddle. "The linemen were on one side and the skill guys were on the other; you had a tight end on one end and the QB on the other. Sometimes the new guys would talk out of turn, and those of us who'd been there a while knew that wouldn't end well," Cross said with a laugh. "Joe would tell them to shut up or, if it was practice, you'd see Bill reiterate that the quarterback is the only person who talks in the huddle. If you have something to say to him, say it after the play before you get in the huddle."

In games when the huddle wasn't orderly—for instance, two players might be arguing about what happened on the previous play—Montana would command their attention with a simple instruction: "Take that to the parking lot." According to Hall of Fame wide receiver Jerry Rice, that was Montana's way of saying, "Enough"—communicating that certain issues weren't important in the heat of the game and could be dealt with later. In the huddle, the focus had to be on the play at hand, not irrelevant differences of opinion. The "parking lot" thus became a figurative place where players went to discuss off-topic matters after important meetings ("huddles").

Montana's discipline didn't mean the huddles were always grimly purposeful, however. His teammates remember that he had a way of lightening the mood in the most intense moments. No other player, they said, could better handle the pressure before a game-winning play or cool the nerves of his teammates as they faced do-or-die situations.

The most famous of these moments occurred during Super Bowl XXIII on January 22, 1989. With just three minutes remaining on the clock and in a nerve-racking huddle, Montana looked at the other end of the field, pointed at a hefty fan, and said, "Isn't that John Candy?" The reference to the comedic actor had the desired effect: Montana's teammates snickered in amusement and relaxed. This simple act loosened the 49ers and allowed them to focus on playing rather than the pressure of the situation. Immediately after that huddle, Montana led the 49ers on a ninety-two-yard, game-winning touchdown drive.

Altogether, Montana's huddles orchestrated thirty-three game-winning drives in his career—tenth most in NFL history. His combination of command and calm in the huddle, precise communication with his supervisor Walsh, and understanding of how to discipline and reassure his teammates were all keys to his team's success. Whether it was telling teammates to "Take that to the parking lot" or cracking a joke at the right moment, Montana kept his huddles efficient and focused and thus provided a competitive advantage for his team.

AND FOR THE TRULY GREAT TEAMS IN BUSINESS

Great Teams in businesses take a cue from Bill Walsh and Joe Montana when it comes to conducting orderly, disciplined meetings. Such order makes a bigger difference than many leaders want to admit.

According to a pair of recent studies by Steven Rogelberg, Chancellor's Professor and professor of management at the University of North Carolina at Charlotte, 37 percent of meetings begin late by an average of fifteen minutes. The studies—which surveyed 480 workers—also found that meeting delays disrupted creativity and hurt job performance. The researchers noted that in organizations that lacked consequences for employee lateness to meetings—which is usually the case—the lateness only *increased* over time.[1]

Ultimately, Rogelberg's studies revealed severe implications for a professional team that loses control over its meetings: its employees will not only dislike and dread those appointments but also harbor growing dissatisfaction with their jobs and the organization itself due to the mismanagement.

A Great Team, therefore, will be intentional about how meetings are conducted. In addition to being orderly, they should also be informative and engaging and, when appropriate, use emotionally driven objectives to reconnect employees to the organization's ultimate purpose—its "why." Phil Lussier, board chairman of the Make-A-Wish Foundation, has described these as "mission moments."

Lussier began his experience with the Make-A-Wish organization (which grants the wishes of children with life-threatening diseases) when his own seriously ill child was granted a wish. Lussier, a financial services executive, subsequently became involved with the foundation. Since then he has regularly arranged mission moments for Make-A-Wish employees and volunteers. At every meeting while he was chair of the national board, for instance, Lussier had a "wish child" or wish family visit and share their Make-A-Wish experience. Such heartfelt moments reminded everyone in the room of the true purpose for their hard work.

Leaders of any thriving organization must always find ways to connect the company mission with employees in a more personal way. Having people and purpose in sync can humble a company and motivate the workforce to strive for even greater success. And meetings are the perfect place to strengthen this connection.

G. J. Hart, CEO of California Pizza Kitchen, considers meetings to be opportunities for leaders to build a "block of trust" by listening to the perspectives of their employees. "I like to create platforms and safe places where people can get together and talk about issues, communicate best practices, and build upon each other," Hart said. "You may not be able to touch everyone, but employee trust and word of mouth is always in support of leaders who listen and learn from their teams."

Hart said that when he joined the organization, he wanted to remove the distance between himself and his front-end team members. So whenever he visited California Pizza Kitchen locations, Hart began initiating impromptu meetings with staff just to say hello and see how things worked behind the scenes. Though surprised at first, his team warmly embraced the opportunity to get to know the CEO and ask questions. Hart said these meetings gave him valuable insight into the day-to-day challenges and needs of those who ran his company.

"I now go around the restaurants, and team members are looking forward to seeing me, discussing best practices or challenges, rather than fearful of an informal CEO visit," he said.

Silicon Valley approaches meetings with a goal of maximizing responsibility, efficiency, and creativity. Apple lists a DRI—or Directly Responsible Individual—beside all items on a meeting agenda in order to clearly determine who does what task. Steve Jobs, former CEO of Apple, would aggressively analyze and question employees and their ideas, and his inquisitive nature embedded itself into Apple's corporate culture. Thus Apple personnel are accustomed to challenging ideas not just in society, but among themselves. Team members who present new ideas to peers in meetings must be willing to aggressively defend those ideas from sharp, honest criticism.[2]

In a 2012 issue of *Think with Google*, Kristen Gil, vice president of business operations and strategy for Google, detailed some of the changes the tech giant instituted when the business became "too large to move quickly." One observation pointed to the company's inefficient running of meetings.

"A well-run meeting is a great thing; it empowers people to make decisions, solve problems, and share information," Gil wrote. "We didn't want our employees to waste either time or energy, so we gathered input and made some recommendations to help make meetings more effective."[3]

One of these recommendations that became policy was to limit meetings to no more than ten people. "Attending meetings isn't a badge of honor," Gil wrote, adding later, "and most importantly, decisions should never wait for a meeting."[4]

Another change made because of employee input was that Google meetings became more objective driven. One clear, important decision is expected at the close of every meeting. Gil said that this was how the Google social network Google+ shipped more than one hundred new features in the first ninety days after its launch, accelerating its growth to more than forty million users.

Additionally, the company brought back its informal "bullpen culture" to its many campuses by creating a designated space for executives to meet for decision making. Gil said this dramatically increased the speed at which ideas became finished concepts.

"The challenges Google faces aren't unique," she wrote. "In a permanently accelerating environment, we're all seeking the best ways to move faster and be smarter."[5]

Running better, more efficient meetings can be an important speed enhancer in any Great Team.

GREAT TAKEAWAYS

A successful meeting revolves around clear communication. It can be pivotal to achieving greatness because it explains precise strategy and opens the door to new ideas. An efficient meeting allows an organization to remain one step ahead of the competition and forces it to remain consistent with any existing strategies. But these ideas must be streamlined by a process and guided by a leader who can filter out the good ideas from the bad.

Here are ten ways Great Teams can ensure equally great meetings:

1. Begin and end meetings on time. Consider instituting consequences for team members who are chronically late.
2. Schedule meetings wisely. Great meetings and huddles are planned when all participants can attend.
3. Begin with a shared or pre-read agenda—and stick to it.
4. Engage employees with strong, emotion-driving content. Meeting agendas tie back into the organization's greater purpose.

5. Make the meeting's objective clear from the beginning. Leaders should state what the meeting should accomplish during the time.
6. Don't waste time with off-topic discussion. Meetings are not social hours or brainstorming sessions.
7. Allot enough time for necessary discussion points.
8. Calculate the cost of all in the meeting and make the appointment count. Remember, time is expensive.
9. Tailor the meetings for all participants.
10. End the meeting by reviewing objectives met or decisions made. Make sure everyone knows the expectations for executing those objectives or decisions.

If a professional team decides to put these lessons into practice in its organization, it is creating a stronger mold for future success. That's what the Great Teams do.

Pillar Four

MUTUAL DIRECTION

CHAPTER 12

GREAT TEAMS IMPROVE THROUGH SCOUTING

They evaluate themselves and their competition to gain a competitive advantage.

Great Teams scout their competition in order to gain competitive advantage. They study the ways their opponents react to challenges and structure themselves for success. Having a clear understanding of how competitors do things can set up a company to do the same things better. This is key for immediate and long-term success.

But successful scouting of competitors is just the beginning. Outside information is of little use unless it's applied. For that reason, professional teams seeking to become industry leaders must evaluate their own behaviors with the same vigor with which they scout other teams. The Great Teams in sports and business keep themselves keenly aware of their teams' potentials and limitations by aggressively studying their own performances and tendencies. Such meticulous self-analysis can reveal potential flaws in even the most airtight of game plans.

In this chapter your team will learn effective ways to evaluate internally and externally and to develop better methods of identifying and improving weaknesses.

GREAT TEAMS IN SPORTS

In sports an appropriate strategy or game plan cannot be formulated without a detailed scouting report. Most teams conduct scouting in a standard way. Advance scouts watch upcoming opponents a few days or even weeks before the scheduled games. Those scouts provide both firsthand and video evaluation of the opponents' tendencies or styles of play. Additionally, the staff completes a computer analysis of the opposing teams—both current and long-term—for the coaches to study and break down.

Though scouting and analysis is common in every major sport, Major League Baseball probably depends on it the most, employing detailed analysis and tracking of almost any situation. A common scouting report in baseball will include details of a rival pitcher's recent injury and how he might change his throwing motion to compensate or how he might tire sooner in the game. These details are used to project how that player is likely to pitch as the game progresses and what pitch he'll throw in certain situations.

Baseball programs will often tailor their entire game plans according to the valuable information yielded in a scouting report. Unbeknownst to many casual fans, "shifting" defense is a popular tactic used by a majority of baseball teams. If a player has a tendency to hit to the left or right, a well-scouted opposing team will overload defensive players to that side of the field, resulting in an easy out.

In the NFL, scouting centers on knowing the play-calling habits of the other team while the next play is developing—a lot of preparation for a brief, intense burst of action. And no one was better at reading these patterns than quarterback Peyton Manning. Manning, who retired in 2016 after a stellar career with the Indianapolis Colts and the Denver Broncos, commanded one of the best-run offenses each season by meticulously scouting his opponents' as well as his own performances.

Manning's game-week preparation tradition began in his first college season, as a third-string quarterback at the University of Tennessee.

He would ask the video coordinator each week for all the game tape from their opponent's previous season. And he studied those tapes diligently, even bringing them with him to the team hotel the night before the game. Pretty soon Manning was bringing more game film on road trips than the Tennessee coaching staff, and his arduous studying (along with his accurate right arm!) led to his becoming the first-string quarterback.

Manning's trend of preparation continued through his professional career, first with the Indianapolis Colts and then at Denver. His younger teammates would tense up whenever they walked by his locker because they had heard stories about him holding pop quizzes on the playbook and strategy. For Manning, scouting wasn't just about the opponent but about his own team as well. He desired to know the weaknesses on his side of the ball, and then he wanted to know how to fix them.

"I think you have to study yourself a lot," Manning said. "It's important as a quarterback to study yourself, your opponent and be sure you're doing the fundamentals and the mechanics right."

When one of his fellow offensive players made a mistake on a play, Manning corrected the mistake before the coaches had a chance to react. And when a receiver joined the Broncos organization through the draft, free agency, or a trade, Manning would call him immediately and schedule time to work on routes and plays they would need to run. To him, scouting was a process with no off-season—an invaluable tool that can help find and correct mistakes long before the competition does.

Herb Brooks, head coach of the 1980 US Olympic hockey team, was also a master at scouting and adjusting his training and game strategies accordingly. In 1979, he earned the honor of coaching Team USA after leading the University of Minnesota to three NCAA titles in the 1970s. Brooks had a vision of what an American Olympic team should look like and how it should play in order to win against the dominant Soviet Union squad, which had won five Olympic titles from 1956 to 1976.

Brooks believed a team did not necessarily need the best players; it needed the *right* ones. While other executives and coaches involved with the US hockey program tried to persuade him to develop an all-star team of the best players in the country, he recruited actively from his Minnesota squad and its bitter rival, the Boston University team, which had won the NCAA title in 1978. Of the twenty players on the roster, nine played at Minnesota and four were from Boston University.

The first step for Brooks was to get those players from rival teams to come together as a team. Though this would pose some difficulties, Brooks reasoned that his strategy would be easier than trying to get a group of all-stars to learn to play as one.

Next, Brooks had to figure out the Soviet style of play. At the time, most considered European hockey to be a finesse game, solely focused on controlling the puck. By contrast, North Americans played a more physical game, with teams trying to overpower one another. The Soviets were a mix of both styles, combining puck control with physicality. They usually dominated games early and then cruised to victory.

Brooks believed the United States, with younger and quicker players, could match up in terms of finesse and eventually win the endurance battle against a Soviet team that had rarely been tested late in games. So Brooks held grueling practices aimed at improving endurance. His main goal was to acclimate his team to playing at a high level past the point of exhaustion.

Brooks' plan was put to the test during exhibitions leading up to the Olympics. In a final exhibition against the Soviets before the start of the Games, the United States lost 10–3. Brooks faced intense scrutiny in the US hockey community at that point. But the US team played far better once the Olympics started, and their coach's plan began to come together.

In the rematch against the Soviets in the semifinals, the United States kept the game close through the first two periods, matching the Soviets both in physical play and in puck control. Brooks's grueling practices had programmed an intrinsic knowledge of the Soviet scheme into his players, which helped them play in perfect cohesion.

With exactly ten minutes of play left, Team USA found themselves leading 4–3. Brooks's extensive scouting had told him that backing off and defending their slim lead would be a mistake. Instead, he instructed the US team to continue attacking the Soviets, forcing them to expend more energy at the defensive end. This was unfamiliar territory to the Soviets, and as the game wore on they began to play with desperation. In fact, they were so ill-prepared for this situation they left their goalie in for the duration of the game, defying the common practice of pulling the goalie in favor of an extra offensive player.

Clearly, the Soviets had never practiced winning a game in the closing minutes. The US team was able to complete what was, arguably, the biggest upset in sports history. ABC sports anchor Jim McKay compared the victory to "an all-star team of Canadian college boys beating the [Super Bowl champion] Pittsburgh Steelers."[1] The cover of *Sports Illustrated* that week featured only a picture of the US team celebrating and no words.[2] The US team went on to win the gold medal in the championship game against Sweden to complete what has been long known as the "Miracle on Ice."

Herb Brooks's scouting paid off. He knew his opponents so well that he forced them into unchartered waters, put them on the defensive, and created advantages for his team. He knew his own players so well that he got them to play an unconventional style together. His insistence on scouting his opponent, evaluating his team, and developing an effective game plan from what he had learned, directly led to Team USA's success.

AND FOR THE TRULY GREAT TEAMS IN BUSINESS

Great Teams have an open perspective when assessing the marketplace. In his widely cited book, *General Management*, J. Kroon writes about "environmental scanning," which he defines as "the study of social, political and technological trends which influence a business, an industry and even a total market."[3] He continues in detail about the value of this kind of scanning and how it can reveal needs and trends in the business ecosystem. When leaders of a professional team perform a scan, they examine the trends dominating their customer demographics, education, government policy, and especially their competition.

Supermarket industry leaders depend on this kind of scouting to remain dominant in a crowded marketplace. In the Southeast region of the United States, Publix Super Markets are well aware of how a competitor can offset their own success. That's why the organization sends its managers to study Walmart Supercenter stores whenever a new location opens up in the vicinity of a Publix. The managers scout prices to remain competitive and to build an advantage over similar products. And the results of these efforts have been stunning: in 2015 Publix maintained a stronghold on the marketplace in the South and, according to the *Tampa Bay Times*, in Florida, where the grocery chain controls 43 percent of the retail grocery business.[4]

Knowing your opponent is a crucial part of emulating and defeating that opponent. But scouting is only the first step. Too many leaders spend countless hours studying an opponent's every move in the search for an edge. The Great Teams understand not only how to scout but also how to exploit the weaknesses of a competitor. These teams analyze every perspective and option and position themselves to take full advantage of any knowledge gained about an opponent.

And once again, external scouting is of limited value if it's not teamed with rigorous self-examination. Successful coaches or managers have learned the value of utilizing an outside opinion to give them a fresh look at their personnel. This unbiased view provides an even greater insight, which in turn helps the coach develop flexibility within the team.

Many businesses use a similar approach to self-scouting. Publix utilizes "mystery shopping," employing "professional shoppers" to visit its stores periodically and give a thorough inspection of each department. The shoppers privately audit for general issues such as timeliness of service and friendliness of staff. They even check to see if the bathrooms are clean. For a store with the motto, "Where shopping is a pleasure,"[5] Publix must make sure it upholds and exceeds industry standards—which is why the supermarket chain consistently rates as one of the best-run companies in the country.

In the corporate world, the SWOT analysis is a user-friendly, widely accepted tool that helps an organization evaluate itself internally. The acronym stands for:

- **S**trengths: factors that give an edge for the company over its competitors
- **W**eaknesses: factors that can be harmful if used against the firm by its competitors
- **O**pportunities: favorable situations which can bring a competitive advantage
- **T**hreats: unfavorable situations which can negatively affect the business[6]

The SWOT analysis allows leaders to take advantage of the insights obtained in their research. Leaders who utilize the SWOT understand that they can directly manage their internal strengths and weaknesses and capitalize on favorable conditions in the marketplace, but must anticipate—and react appropriately to—outside threats.

Amazon.com, the world's largest online retailer, has used the SWOT analysis since it opened its virtual doors in 1995. Since then, the company's low cost structure and large merchandise selection have generated billions in online sales; in 2014, Amazon earned more than $80 billion online. A collection of 2015 Amazon SWOT reports revealed a number of impressive strengths, such as superior selection of products and services, strategic company acquisitions, an efficient distribution system, and economic strength.

Amazon's operation as an online store gives it economic leverage since it doesn't have a cost for running physical outlets. This is also Amazon's number-one weakness, however; by being solely an online store, it cannot compete with the immersive experience of rival retailers Walmart and Target. After years of SWOT analysis, Amazon made the decision in 2015 to begin opening physical stores at select locations, creating new challenges and opportunities.

The company also suffers from negative publicity regarding its questionable tax avoidance in the United States and United Kingdom, where its revenues are the highest. Reports of poor warehouse conditions, strong-arm tactics to gain market share, and price discrimination also show up in the weakness column. As for threats, cybersecurity issues always loom. Amazon faces several substantial lawsuits, and strategic alliances among other e-commerce giants could pose a threat as well.

But Amazon CEO Jeff Bezos—one of the world's richest people—is confident in Amazon turning its problems into strengths. In 2015 its Web Services division added 530 new features and thirty thousand robots in its warehouses, doubling its number from last year—and all with an end goal of innovation.[7]

"This is one more step in our mission to bring customers premium products at non-premium prices," Bezos said in *Bloomberg Business*.[8]

Benchmarking, like the SWOT analysis, is one of a leader's strongest resources in identifying how the company's products, practices, and services measure up against competitors. The goal of benchmarking is to evaluate whether internal processes are above or below external industry standards. This works by examining company-to-company comparisons of day-to-day functions and overall performance.

Benchmarking not only reveals key weaknesses. It can also improve programs, expose productivity gaps, motivate employees, and support quality improvement.

Xerox, a company that first put the photocopier on the market and monopolized the industry for many years, lost huge portions of its market in the late 1970s because of innovations by IBM and Kodak. Additionally, Canon, Ricoh, and Savin were beating the company in low-end sales. To counter this distressing situation, Xerox leadership instituted a process of internal and external review that would eventually be called *benchmarking*.

Surprisingly, many of its executives resisted the new approach. Few wanted to believe that the company—a giant in the print and photocopier world—was failing in most of its processes. But the initial resistance eventually turned to action. After careful scrutiny, the company made dramatic changes. It reduced national suppliers by the thousands, eliminated layers of hierarchical leadership, and made team building a part of company culture. As a result, Xerox cut down on quality problems, reduced its manufacturing costs by half, and shortened its developmental process. Additionally, Xerox cut direct labor within its staff by 50 percent while increasing volume and production.[9]

Xerox saved the company with benchmarking.

GREAT TAKEAWAYS

Knowing your opponents is essential to successfully outperforming them. To create an appropriate business strategy that stays ahead of the competition, everyone in the organization must understand how competitors operate and how to use that knowledge to their advantage. Leaders must understand the importance scouting plays within their organizations as well as knowing their teams' strengths and struggles. During the process of internal scouting, ideas may regularly surface that never have been considered before—including the possibility of empowering team members with new positions of responsibility.

But simply knowing isn't enough. As Xerox's example showed, knowledge obtained through internal or external scouting must also be accepted and used as the basis for change.

A Great Team identifies the variety of options it has in self-scouting, such as the SWOT analysis and benchmarking. By knowing and using the tools available, a company has a better chance of employing the right people at the right time. All perspectives should be taken into consideration; a fresh look by an unbiased evaluator can be especially helpful in revealing blind spots.

When examining opponents, Great Teams identify tendencies and habits that can be exploited. As with Herb Brooks and Team USA, productive self-evaluation begins by learning your weaknesses and those of your opponents in order to develop both an offensive and defensive game plan to outplay your competition.

Scouting—both internal and external—is a consistent learning tool that all teams should adopt and reinforce. Good scouting keeps a team continually aware of its potential, the capabilities of its opponents, and the need to develop aggressive championship strategies.

CHAPTER 13

GREAT TEAMS SEE VALUE OTHERS MISS

They use analytics to think outside the box.

G reat teams never answer the "why" question with, "Because we've always done it this way." Instead, they regularly evaluate each situation and seek unique opportunities for improvement. In today's fast-paced world, many of those opportunities can be found in the world of *analytics*—defined as "the method of logical analysis."

Big data is a hot topic in the worlds of sports and business because the collection of metrics, analytics, and information can reveal a potential advantage or disadvantage. The Great Teams collect that data and analyze it to recognize trends others might miss. Analytics can supply teams with a fresh set of goggles through which to look at their current environments and discover areas where teams can make major advancements.

In this chapter you will be challenged to find innovative ways to enhance your team by using this wide-open mind-set to your advantage.

GREAT TEAMS IN SPORTS

Sports franchises, like multibillion-dollar corporations, find success through efficiently utilizing the resources available to them. In many cases, financial restrictions have actually helped build championship teams through traditional methods such as player drafts. Over the past three decades, overwhelmingly, NBA titles have been won by organizations that made strategic use of salary cap space that comes from deftly selecting the right talent. Magic Johnson, Larry Bird, Isiah Thomas, Michael Jordan, Hakeem Olajuwon, and Kobe Bryant, to name a few, were all franchise players acquired through the draft.

But one of the most innovative streaks in recent years came via a different route. In 2003 the Detroit Pistons began a six-season run of success. Every season they at least reached the NBA Eastern Conference championship round. They made the finals twice and captured an NBA championship in 2004. The streak was even more impressive in light of the fact that the Pistons roster consisted of league castoffs. Four of Detroit's five starting players had been acquired either in free agency or trade.

This motley crew included guards Chauncey Billups and Richard Hamilton, the short-tempered Rasheed Wallace—who led the NBA in technical fouls—and defensive and rebounding champ Ben Wallace, who possessed little talent for scoring. While considered good by most NBA analysts, each player had defects in his individual game. Only once in that six-year run did any player—Richard Hamilton—even average twenty points per game over a whole season.

And yet the value of the Pistons as a whole was more than the sum of its individual parts. Together the players formed a machine of consistency, a cohesive unit that played impeccable defense and fed off each other on offense.

General manager Joe Dumars, who had played on Detroit's previous title-winning teams in the 1990s with Isiah Thomas, was among the first in the league to recognize how a cohesive unit could be built with players rejected by other teams. But Dumars also knew he had to be careful with spending money; the Pistons couldn't simply go out and buy the best available players in free agency. So Dumars set out to build his team culture by finding available talent at low cost—and, he hoped, finding players with chips on their shoulders.

This strategy made all the difference in a league full of free-agent-riddled teams with pricey contracts and zero chemistry. The Pistons developed a team based on the resources available and found success. With his ragtag team of players, Dumars seized upon the hurt pride and desire of the Pistons and created NBA champions.

Sometimes a team needs a fresh look at what everyone has decided the "rules" for success look like. At the Pulaski Academy, a prep school in Little Rock, Arkansas, the Bruins varsity football team is led by one of the great innovators in all of football—Coach Kevin Kelley. In 2003, Coach Kelley watched an old VHS tape of a lecture by a Harvard professor on the value of the fourth-down punt. The professor analyzed two thousand football games and came to the conclusion that teams should *never* punt the ball.[1]

Prompted by this notion, Coach Kelley questioned the reasoning behind every football decision the Bruins made. The first and most profound question was, "Why exactly do we punt on fourth down?" The short answer, Kelley found, was "because everybody else does." But armed with new perspective and valuable stats, Kelley broke down the numbers behind his own team's fourth-down decisions. The data he found backed up the concept that going for it on fourth down was the correct call, even though most football coaches adamantly insisted on punting the ball to the other team.

And for that reason, the Pulaski Academy Bruins made an unorthodox decision: they would never punt the football again. The approach proved effective for Coach Kelley's team; they've converted half of all fourth-down attempts since this decision, giving Coach Kelley flexibility on his play calling and more opportunities to score during the game. The Bruins have also begun to use third downs as an opportunity to shorten the distance of its upcoming fourth down attempts.

Coach Kelley's unconventional football philosophy has been effective for his team, which has five state championships under his leadership.[2]

Across the country in Concord, California, Bob Ladouceur, former head coach of the most successful high school football dynasty in American history—the De La Salle Spartans—amassed an incredible 399 wins, twenty perfect seasons, and an undefeated streak from 1992 to 2004. "Coach Lad" had mastered the art of scouting, which allowed him to breathe new life each year into a championship team that had dominated the year before.

It's a feat that even the most accomplished sports and business leaders have been unable to attain. And yet Coach Lad sustained dominance with a roster of sixteen-year-olds, season after season, with "commitment cards" and a culture of accountability.

Each week during his tenure, Ladouceur would pair up his players and have them write down their conditioning, practice, and game goals on the cards and recite them to their commitment partners. The goals had to be specific and measurable, so that the team could evaluate as a whole whether or not each member had delivered on his commitment. Players who failed to live up to their commitments would have to explain to the team why they were not successful.

"The idea behind the commitment cards was that I wanted my players to be responsible to each other and understand that their contributions impact the team as a whole," Ladouceur shared with me during an interview. "For many of them—for a lot of people, actually—making a commitment to your teammate is completely outside-the-box thinking. The beauty of football is that you have so many guys. But one or two can destroy the entire team if they aren't pulling their weight. I wanted my players to understand that if they were going to be a member of any team, then they would have to stay accountable to each another, on and off the field."

This incredible leadership tool helped Ladouceur's players analyze themselves and others and make adjustments if necessary. Furthermore, the self-scouting fit into the overall culture of De La Salle High, where visitors would not find any championship trophy displays or all-time record listings of the Spartan's incredible accomplishments. "We didn't really care about visual acknowledgments of achievement," Coach Lad said, "because it was secondary to the humility and commitment of personal excellence that our team stood for."

Ladouceur admitted that when it came to teaching life lessons, the coach's voice was not as effective as a fellow teammate's, which could be "a driver for success."

"I think the voice of a peer has more power than any authority figure or coach," Coach Lad said. "And when our players started challenging each other to be better, the discipline and character of our team grew stronger."

The commitments the students made when playing football for Coach Lad often became game changers for life. Long after they graduated, the majority of his players kept their cards close as reminders to always live up to the commitments they had made to those who believed in them.

"There's no such thing as perfection in life or athletics," Coach Ladouceur said. "There's always going to be mistakes and letdowns. So I used the commitment cards as a vehicle to teach peace, humility, and to show that no one will ever be perfect. There is always room for improvement."

Financial strain can limit an organization's ability to bring in top-tier talent, but money isn't always the most important factor in building a Great Team. Billy Beane, who became general manager for the Oakland Athletics in 1987, found that the organization's chronically poor finances forced him to be creative in structuring his team. But that creativity would be tested when he lost three star players—Jason Giambi, Johnny Damon, and Jason Isringhausen—to free agency after the 2001 Major League Baseball season.

Giambi had been the American League's MVP in 2000, Damon was the team's leadoff hitter, and Isringhausen was a star closer. The A's lost all of them because they simply couldn't afford them. As a result, many analysts and fans dismissed the A's and assumed that their replacements would be incapable of filling the void in the team.

Instead, Oakland nearly became the World Series champions thanks to Beane's use of sabermetrics, or the application of statistical analysis to baseball records, to evaluate and compare the performance of individual players. Professional baseball is a great laboratory for using statistics to predict behavior, because the long, 162-game season provides a lot of data to be analyzed. Beane, though, knew he had to see those statistics with new eyes.

The groundwork for this success story, depicted in the bestselling book *Moneyball* and the movie by the same name,[3] was laid in 1995, when new ownership took over the A's and ordered general manager Sandy Alderson and Beane, then assistant general manager, to slash payroll to ensure the team's profitability. Beane, whom Stanford University had recruited for a joint baseball-football scholarship before he decided to turned pro in baseball, had to find alternative strategies in order to compete. So he began to study sabermetrics to come up with trends that might prove beneficial. In 1999, Beane hired Paul DePodesta to be his assistant general manager. DePodesta had also played both baseball and football and had graduated from Harvard with a degree in economics.

Beane and DePodesta first looked at Scott Hatteberg, a player released by the Boston Red Sox after he failed to produce as a catcher. But the A's realized that while Hatteberg was a mediocre catcher, he had a tendency to get on base regularly. In sabermetric verbiage, he had a high on-base percentage. He could score more runs because statistically he could get on base more often.

Oakland also used research to determine that collegiate athletes were better picks for their organization than high school players. Most college players were older and were more experienced against advanced competition. Their major-league performance was easier to predict, and they were cheaper and more productive in the long run. Most college players were ready to cash in once drafted, as compared to high school players, who readily used the idea of going to college as leverage for more money.

Together, Beane and DePodesta revolutionized professional team management. While most scouts viewed baseball through a prism of raw talent, using intuition and historical comparisons to predict a player's performance, Beane and DePodesta put emphasis on measurable stats such as on-base percentage and slugging percentage. By relying on data instead, applying Wall Street–style business planning to building a franchise, and competing under the limits of a less-than-optimal payroll, the A's became one of the most efficient teams in baseball. Their ability to identify their players' individual strengths allowed many of them to succeed quickly. As a result, in 2002 the A's won an American League record of twenty straight games and finished the season with a 103–59 record in the regular season. While they never won a World Series under Beane's leadership, the A's produced a consistently competitive team despite being one of the lowest-revenue organizations in the league.

AND FOR THE TRULY GREAT
TEAMS IN BUSINESS

The Oakland A's use of sabermetrics reflects a trend that has revolutionized business as well. The corporate world has embraced statistics as a way of building professional teams and supercharging transactional relationships with consumers. With metrics now considered a best practice in today's marketplace, several key lessons have emerged from the leading voices in statistical analysis:

Big data drives accurate decision making. Statisticians understand the importance of informed business decisions, and data analysis can help encourage an organization toward—or dissuade it from—taking a course of action. The Orlando Magic organization uses data to invest resources into making better decisions about not just basketball but also marketing. Using analytics, the Magic can analyze the habits and purchasing trends of the many tourists who visit their city in a given year. With this information, the organization can dip into the bustling tourism market and attract new consumers.

"Data is of key importance when we make our business decisions.

In some instances it may be the driving factor, and in some decisions it may be just a consideration point as we are going through the decision-making process," said Jay Riola, director of business strategy for the Orlando Magic. "We are fortunate to not only have great people who work in strategy and analytics, but also to have great people throughout the organization who recognize the value and importance of informed decision making. And a lot of times that requires going back to customer-level data or ticketing data and using that information to help guide the decision and do what's best for the company, for the fan across the board."

Riola and his organization use this stat-driven decision making to enhance the experiences of fans who visit Amway Center in Orlando for a Magic game. For them, interpreting data correctly has a direct effect on their customers and downstream beneficiaries.

"We use customer data to inform our interactions with you and provide relevant experiences and offers that matter to you," Riola said to me. "So if you are a family member or you're there for personal or business—whatever reasons you might be at the game—we use the information we have on you to customize your experience. How we interact with you ultimately improves your experience and builds the relationship with our team."

Predictive statistics can be highly profitable. Businesses that utilize statistics are more profitable because their collected data can be mined for all sorts of valuable information—such as improving and maximizing transactions.

The St. Louis Cardinals are exceptional with using data in this way and have utilized predictive statistics to overshadow the St. Louis Rams, the NFL team that played there until 2016. Football is America's biggest sport, and in every market where an NFL and MLB coexist, the football team is more popular with citizens. But not in St. Louis. The Cardinals organization tapped into predictive statistics to build an incredible fan base in the St. Louis region. This in turn influenced the local culture; twice as many people in St. Louis play baseball or softball in comparison to any other MLB and NFL market.

"Every industry is addicted to predictive analytics because it allows you to get a better sense of how to sell more, sell efficiently and quicker," said Rich Luker, creator of the ESPN Sports Poll. The poll measures sports fan interests, activities, and preferences in the United States and has become a fixture in pop culture. "So when we treat sports like it's a transaction, it's evident that we are selling experience and relationship. Fans buy a relationship, and unless they have a relationship with the team, there's no reason for them to buy the hotdogs or the shirts. So the focus in sports has to first be on relationships."

Predictive statistics can also be an important long-term growth piece for an organization. "The only way you are going to have people buying from you twenty years from now is to have a relationship, and predictive analytics ensures that," Luker said.

Statistics help teams relate more with customers. Data can bridge the gap between a consumer and an organization and can offer ample opportunities to create profitable business connections.

"If you can relate to a consumer and their demographic, then you know their other behavioral attributes that determine what they are likely to do with your product," said David Smrek, vice president for LiveAnalytics, a division of Ticketmaster International. Smrek and his team of statisticians and researchers provide fan data to sports teams and the country's biggest venues. "The better the communication with that customer or that prospect, the better the chances are that the customer will seek out your product in the future. If we can show you that we care about the same things [as you] and make good usage of a customer's time, then ultimately we'll be more successful in leading them toward a desired outcome for us."

Statistics can help market to targeted groups. For Rick Johnson, vice president and general manager of the Pricemaster division at Live Nation Entertainment, analytics has revolutionized the live entertainment industry in the past five years—particularly the corporate side.

"Analytics plays a huge role in everything from pricing and marketing to building relationships with your customers and making important connections," Johnson said. "Companies are increasing revenue streams by 30 percent by some remarkably simple things, and we've started to add a broad spectrum of marketing and pricing to structure products into packages for our specific demographics."

Marketing products differently to different groups helps a company target messaging to consumers and really cater to their needs. "Customers are not one monolithic entity," Johnson said. "Really targeting your messaging to different segments of your customer base and thinking about them critically is very important because they aren't all the same."

In the live entertainment industry, there is a huge spectrum of consumers that Johnson says can be better served by tailoring marketing efforts to their specific needs—such as frequent concertgoers who seek out the best seats or families who only come to one or two events a year and are looking to make economic decisions.

"You have to message the millennial differently versus the fifty-five-year-old executive and men versus women," Johnson said. "A unique message for each audience resonates more with consumers."

GREAT TAKEAWAYS

Being resource efficient is a nonnegotiable goal for businesses. But realizing how to operate efficiently is more important, even if businesses must take a risk by employing out-of-the-box tactics. Corporations need to build teams in ways that benefit the organization as a whole, as opposed to centering on individual achievement. Teams that look for value in areas that the competition ignores will almost always gain the competitive advantage.

Anson Dorrance, head coach for the highly successful University of North Carolina women's soccer team, says that big-data evaluations on player performance are "an unquestionable method of fostering depth and discovering new leaders."

"One of the best things about having data drive performance is when you are sitting in a player conference with the players across your desk and they're looking at their practice performance data," Dorrance said. "Just seeing their own performance displayed before them is a motivator to improve."

Like the Oakland A's and the Detroit Pistons, teams can use unconventional methods to compete against opponents with greater resources. Unorthodox advantages are available to all teams, but the Great Teams— like the Pulaski Academy Bruins or De La Salle Spartans—find a way to use those advantages effectively. Great Teams use all of their skills to tap into and find hidden value within their personnel. Innovative change doesn't typically happen overnight, however. Team leaders must be patient while their groundbreaking strategies take root and develop within team culture.

Any team desiring to be great should not ignore the value of analytics. Whether consumers are interacting with mobile applications or purchasing tickets at the box office, they will inevitably leave a trail of data that can be captured and leveraged for maximizing customer experience and meeting their needs with better offerings. The sooner business owners and team leaders understand this reality, the more predictable their competitive advantages become. But even if a team isn't regularly using analytics to predict behavior, data can still drive decisions that save the organization time, money, and undue stress.

There is no need to reinvent the wheel when it comes to analytics. These innovative data collection programs already exist for much of the sports and business world. With a little creativity, persistence, and an attitude of turning disadvantages into motivation, a team can use data to become great at meeting customer demands through innovation. But to do that—to become a Great Team—it must use this data to find value that others miss.

CHAPTER 14

GREAT TEAMS WIN IN CRITICAL SITUATIONS

They thrive and win in high-pressure circumstances.

Every player or employee wants to be a part of a team that can achieve victory in the most critical of situations. A Great Team wins in those moments because it has figured out effective ways to finish strong. And with the game on the line, a team accustomed to pressure can execute its strategy without hesitation *and* not fall apart in the process.

The Great Teams in sports and business have developed cultures that emphasize this need to finish strong. They understand that if they let up on the competition at the wrong time, then they open up opportunities for failure. These are teams that never coast.

Maintaining a lead in sports or business comes down to consistency. Even when a Great Team is running ahead of the competition, it musters the discipline never to celebrate prematurely. And when the competition is neck and neck and victory is on the line, Great Teams refuse to shrink from the challenge. The culture of a fourth-quarter team requires countless hours of team preparation so that its members learn to trust in themselves and each other when the stakes are high. This type of approach can help a team get through a season, series, or game even when the scoreboard tilts the wrong way.

The history of sports is packed with examples of people who handled the pressure of the end-game scenarios and came out winners. NFL quarterbacks Johnny Unitas, Roger Staubach, John Elway, and Tom

Brady have built reputations based on their coolness in the fourth quarter. Likewise, Robert Horry of the Los Angeles Lakers and San Antonio Spurs was one of the greatest clutch performers in the NBA playoffs. Horry was so calm in critical situations that he became known by the end of his career as "Big Shot Bob." This sense of calm and confidence, like all habits of Great Teams, is driven by culture as well as personality and training. It is carefully developed in an organization's huddles, meetings, and practices.

The late Jim Tracy, former head coach of San Francisco's University High School women's cross-country team, was the most successful coach of his sport in California. Tracy regularly reminded his athletes that life is about finishing strong, and his team translated this message into winning ten state titles—the most in California history.

In 2010, Tracy was diagnosed with amyotrophic lateral sclerosis—better known as Lou Gherig's Disease—a neurological disease that attacks the nervous system, causing excruciating pain and eventual paralysis. But Tracy hardly ever took a day off, even as his body deteriorated. He even led his team to two state championships from a wheelchair. Tracy's physical sacrifice and message of resilience had an incredible impact on his athletes, who used his example as fuel to always find the strength to end the race.

That unique relationship was on display at the 2010 California state cross-country meet, where Tracy's team captain Holland Reynold's perseverance made her an overnight sports sensation. At third place, Reynolds began to tire and slow. She had critically misjudged her hydration before the race. With three yards left before the finish line, Reynolds pitched forward and crashed into the grass.

"Right after I collapsed, an official came over to me, and he let me know that if I wanted to finish the race, I had to either get up and walk through or crawl through, but he couldn't help me right then, or else I'd be disqualified," Reynolds said in an ESPN short feature, *The Finish Line*.[1]

But not finishing was not a part of Reynolds's team's culture.

So she began to crawl.

Slowly, on hands and knees, Reynolds muscled through the pain and utter exhaustion to cross the finish line. Though she finished in thirty-seventh place, her tenacity sent a clear message: *No matter what, don't quit.* And by not giving in, she gave her team enough points to win the state championship.

Reynolds's effort was indicative of the values taught to her team by Tracy. Even with the championship and her personal health on the line, she demonstrated true commitment to team in a crucial moment.

Former New York Giants head coach Tom Coughlin is famous for his strict discipline and his enforcement of both dedication and leadership. He even created a team policy that fines players—and employees—if they do not arrive at team meetings five minutes early. Coughlin's example has mired itself in the culture of the Giants, and the spirit of dedication within the team has resulted in some of the most memorable clutch performances in the history of the NFL.

During Super Bowl XLII on February 3, 2008, Giants quarterback Eli Manning famously led an improbable drive at the end of the game. That drive, which featured a stunning ball-to-helmet catch by wide receiver David Tyree, won the Giants its third championship title. The shocking loss upset the Patriots' quest for not only a Super Bowl but an undefeated season.

At the beginning of the 2011–2012 season, Coughlin was inspired by Holland Reynolds and flew her out to New York to speak with his team. He adopted the motto "Finish" for the Giants' season and demanded full momentum from his team in every challenge that was to come—no matter what.

Later that season the Giants were tied with the Dallas Cowboys for the division lead and needed to win the last game of the season to make the playoffs. The Cowboys had faded during the season and, as they entered the game with the Giants, were coming off three losses in the last four games. The Giants were carrying momentum from their previous victory over the New York Jets, but the team still needed improvement. With the season on the line, Coach Coughlin reminded his players of their commitment to "finish" and asked them to give their full effort and concentration in order to move forward.

Manning again showed up when needed, throwing for 346 yards and three touchdowns to capture a crucial 31–14 win over Dallas.

"I knew we were going to fight and keep playing until the end. I feel good about the way we're handling the ups and downs, and it comes down to finishing," Manning said. "My dad just told me, 'Don't change your personality. The reason you have had success and deal with things the way you do is because you don't let a whole lot get to you.'"

Once the playoffs started, the Giants continued to dominate, beating Atlanta 24–2 in the first round, defeating the defending Super Bowl champion Green Bay Packers on the road, and narrowly winning the NFC championship game against the San Francisco 49ers with an overtime field goal.

Coming into Super Bowl XLVI, the stakes and drama couldn't have been higher. The Giants faced a rematch between the 13–3 New England Patriots—who were seeking their fourth Super Bowl win. The Giants shot to a 9–0 lead in the first quarter, and confidence was high. The Patriots fired back, however, scoring seventeen unanswered points and taking a 17–9 lead during the third quarter.

But Coughlin and his resilient team had prepared for these kinds of moments and did not falter, despite what the scoreboard said. The Giants defense adjusted and prevented the Patriots from scoring again, and the Giants' special teams contributed two consecutive field goals to chop away New England's lead to 17–15 at the end of the third quarter.

With less than three minutes to play in the fourth quarter and the teams locked in a stalemate, the Patriots clung to their advantage and refused to fold. But the Giants broke through the Patriots' suffocating defense when Manning completed a thirty-eight-yard pass to Mario Manningham, who had beaten two defenders and was barely in bounds when he caught the ball. The play marked the beginning of an eighty-eight-yard drive that ended with running back Ahmad Bradshaw tumbling into the end zone with fifty-seven seconds remaining on the clock. The comeback had been hard fought, but the Giants were Super Bowl champions once again.

Coughlin later revealed, "We had this goal to finish, finish, finish, and win the fourth quarter."

The winning drive was a far cry from the frenetic finisher that the Giants had gone through to defeat the Patriots four years earlier, but the victory solidified Coughlin's team as one of the strongest in the NFL, capable of handling the most intense situations in the pursuit of ultimate victory.

And across the country, Holland Reynolds was smiling.

In the 2015 NCAA men's basketball championship game, the Duke Blue Devils—led by head coach Mike Krzyzewski—defeated the University of Wisconsin Badgers 68–63 in the final minutes of the game. Krzyzewski said that the secret to his team's victory was "trusting in the judgment of his team and staff," which made all the difference between winning and losing.

One of the biggest challenges for Duke during that game was locking down opposing forward and Naismith Player of the Year Frank Kaminsky, who had a standout game that night with twenty-one points and twelve rebounds. The game was a dead heat until backup guard Grayson Allen scored ten key points in the second half, jolting the Blue Devils with a fresh energy to win. Allen was hot from the field and bold in the inside, often driving to the rim against stronger and taller Badger defenders. During one mismatched moment, Allen let out an emotional outburst after scoring with a one-handed layup. His reaction summarized the entire Duke mentality: be yourself and play with unrelenting passion.

"That's how we won our fifth national championship," Krzyzewski said. "Grayson was our eighth man, and he felt comfortable being himself in that moment. He won the game because he changed the emotional environment; he got Jahlil Okafor and Justise Winslow to stop thinking about their foul trouble, made Matt Jones get more intense in his defense, and Amile Jefferson to volunteer to guard Kaminsky."

Krzyzewski even admits that Grayson helped him to change his own way of thinking, since he'd been keenly observing his players and saw they were all holding back for respective reasons. But with Grayson's reaction, he realized the game was no longer about strategy but culture.

"It was the biggest moment that I have been a part of because we needed a change in our environment, and Grayson used our culture to do it," Krzyzewski shared with me. "Culture is what won us our fifth national championship."

Like the New York Giants, the 2004 Boston Red Sox staged one of the greatest comebacks in sports history by not allowing a challenging situation to overwhelm them.

In the American League Championship Series, the Red Sox faced the New York Yankees, yet another entry into the most storied rivalry in sports. The winner would earn a place in the World Series.

The Red Sox sputtered against the high-performing Yankees, who won convincingly in Games 1 and 2 at New York. The series moved to Boston for Game 3, but not even the home crowd could will the Red Sox to a win as they got thumped by a score of 19–8. Team morale began to drop.

To most outsiders, that embarrassing game was the final nail in the coffin for the Red Sox. No team in baseball history had ever come back from 0–3 deficit in a best-of-seven series. However, the Red Sox were an unusually mature team. They were managed by Terry Francona, the son of a major league player and a player himself in both college and the majors before beginning his career as a coach. Francona believed that no situation was beyond hope.

The Yankees seemed poised to sweep the series in Game 4, but in a seesaw game, New York went into the bottom of the ninth with a one-run lead and had pitcher Mariano Rivera on the mound to close the game. Rivera was on his way to becoming the greatest closer in the history of baseball, but this wasn't going to be his moment. The Red Sox tied the game with the help of a stolen base by pinch runner Dave Roberts, shifting the momentum for the Red Sox. Shortly after Roberts's gutsy move, David Ortiz won the game with a home run in the twelfth inning.

Game 5 of the series brought even more drama when Boston scored two runs in the bottom of the eighth inning. The game went to extra innings before Ortiz again won the game with a home run. Boston's momentum continued even as the series returned to New York, where the team tied the series with a 4–2 win in Game 6.

In the clubhouse after the game, winning pitcher Curt Schilling wore a T-shirt printed with Boston's slogan for the season: "Why Not Us?"

In Game 7, the Red Sox dominated, winning 10–3, and completed the most stunning turnaround of a series in sports history.

The momentum from finishing strong in that series carried the Red Sox to the World Series championship that year.

AND FOR THE TRULY GREAT TEAMS IN BUSINESS

A crisis that threatens an organization isn't usually seen as a pathway into greatness, but that's exactly what happened to health-care company Johnson & Johnson during the fall of 1982. That year the company's Tylenol brand of painkiller was the most successful over-the-counter product in the country and, thanks to its more than one hundred million users, accounted for 19 percent of Johnson & Johnson's profits. Tylenol had outsold all of the combined sales of market competitors Anacin, Bayer, and Excedrin and was the undisputed king of its industry until tragedy shook the company to its core.[2]

Malevolent opportunists in the Chicago area laced Tylenol Extra

Strength capsules with cyanide, resealed the products, and placed the tampered bottles on shelves in a half-dozen stores around the city, causing seven deaths. With a media storm brewing and paranoia high, Johnson & Johnson management found itself in the nightmare scenario of having to explain why its well-known and trusted product was killing people.

Refusing to fold under pressure, Johnson & Johnson chairman James Burke decided to put together a strategic team to answer the immediate, pressing questions regarding Tylenol—how to protect the public and save the product. Consumers were instructed through the media not to use any Johnson & Johnson painkilling products until the tampering had been investigated and resolved. Additionally, the company set up a hotline so the concerned public and media could phone in for daily, prerecorded updates. For Tylenol, this was a powerful method of controlling communications and dispelling rumors.

The damage control didn't stop with open communication; Tylenol halted its advertising, and the company removed all of its products nationwide after two more contaminated bottles were found. The product removal decision and Tylenol's insistence on protecting the public even at the expense of losing millions in profits countered the negative press and earned the company much-needed respect. Public opinion shifted. Instead of being considered a negligent company, the company was now thought of as the victim of a heinous crime.

Building off of that good momentum, the company gained more positive media by holding live press conferences at its corporate headquarters. Burke provided even more transparency when he went on *60 Minutes* and the *Phil Donahue Show* to communicate the company's objectives to America. In response to the tampering, he unveiled the company's new triple-safety-seal packaging—the first in its industry to do so—which consisted of a glued box, plastic wrapping, and a seal over the bottle opening.

Tylenol had not solicited much press coverage before its emergency, but the crisis provided Johnson & Johnson with a rare opportunity to spread information, show resolve, and change the market culture with an innovation. In doing so, the company established a stronger, more positive relationship with key stakeholders and the media, and its approach to crisis management restored public confidence in the company's integrity.

In following years, Tylenol amazingly recovered its market share and regained its spot as a dominant industry leader. By handling a critical situation in a transparent, strategic, and commanding manner, Johnson & Johnson bounced back from the brink of destruction and reasserted itself as a Great Team.

GREAT TAKEAWAYS

For Great Teams, finishing strong and performing under pressure requires inspiration, confidence, and guidance from a focused leader. And great leaders motivate their employees to push through a tough time by helping them realize their jobs are meaningful. This means promoting achievement, recognition, responsibility, and growth. Inspired team members will fight to the very end for their teams.

The solution lies in connecting your team emotionally to the organization's culture by helping them appreciate the value of what they are doing. In a study of workplace enthusiasm by the National Opinion Research Center at the University of Chicago, researchers found that the real-world significance of a person's work ranked highest in terms of what employees said mattered the most to them about their jobs. Interestingly, the study also revealed that those same employees mistakenly believed that money was the highest motivator for their colleagues—but not for them: 75 percent of respondents said incentives in pay were needed to get people to work hard, and 66 percent reported that their peers would not take on additional work tasks unless they were paid to do so.[3]

Many companies mistake movement for momentum. By paying employees to work harder, organizations also create an incentive bias when trying to motivate a strong finish. Paying someone to do more gets movement but not always true motivation. And teams with higher motivation will always beat teams that only get movement.

The NORC study reinforces the reality that our perception of money as a motivator is vastly different from fact. Dispelling this myth is crucial to success. Leaders must realize that their employees want meaning from their work, not just money.

Additionally, during a crisis, a team should emphasize three levers: culture (which brings a team closer together), training, and true incentives that elevate its members and inspire performance. According to a study by the Florida State University Sales Institute, Great Teams who use all three of these levers have an amazing 100 percent success rate when completing objectives during a critical moment.[4]

Finishing strong also requires good conditioning. Great Teams realize that their opponents and customers know about clutch performance as well, but they don't assume that all will go according to plan. Like the New York Giants, teams that win condition themselves by practicing end-of-game strategy. Constant drilling prepares a team to be confident in the tasks that await and to be in great shape to respond to any crisis. During these moments, a team can discover its best strategies, which ones need improvement, and how best to respond to unexpected challenges.

Even though teams work better with collaboration, leaders can mistakenly push their teams further apart by adding new responsibilities—"Let's try this new idea!"—when the going gets tough. According to a study by the *McKinsey Quarterly*, only 30 percent of teams hit their goals when they received unique tasks in pressurized situations.[5] To finish strong, businesses need to have the confidence in themselves to succeed with the full trust and effort of team members. Additionally, a leader must exhibit strength and confidence, as these qualities can become infectious to teammates.

Here are five keys that will help an organization prepare to win in the most critical of situations:

1. Practice and conditioning. The last quarter may require conditioning for the long hours and tough conversations. Get rest and stay ready. Additionally, the extra practice yielded by all that prep time will help a team think more clearly and perform better in critical times.

2. Prioritize. Leaders should determine what impacts their teams' ability to close deals. Though the pressure may increase, leaders should not allow the situation to become bigger than it needs to be.

3. Evaluate status with clients. A high-performing team does not remove its foot from the accelerator even in critical moments but instead focuses on ongoing strategy and goal completion.

4. Play to your strengths. In critical times, a team should always do what it does best. Intense moments should never be the stage for trying something rarely practiced.

5. Create and celebrate mini goals. Team leadership can approach a large-scale goal by breaking it down into more manageable pieces. As the team completes these smaller goals and celebrates progress, accomplishment will set into the workflow and culture.

By considering certain aspects of a team's performance, leaders can identify areas that are key to finishing victoriously. In these preparatory moments, a team can determine the weapons at its disposal, compare how they match up against the competition, and target specific areas needing to be improved.

But none of these strategies will be helpful if a team does not have a great sense of faith in itself to succeed. Ultimately, prevailing during a critical moment comes down to team culture and being ready for that last-minute surge. This approach can help a team deliver an epic win during the most trying of circumstances.

CHAPTER 15

GREAT TEAMS SPEAK A DIFFERENT LANGUAGE

They speak success into existence.

Through success or failure, great leaders always know what to say to bring out the best in their organizations. Many teams under-value the art of properly framing communication, especially in times of struggle. Successful leaders do not berate or chide team members but seek ways to positively articulate objectives and expectations. They have better coaching conversations, ask better questions, and drive results. Positive communication is not only a habit for high-performance teams but also a tool used to reinforce and enhance the values of organizations.

GREAT TEAMS IN SPORTS

Some of the greatest coaches in sports—and leaders in business—have been making a pilgrimage of sorts the last several years to America's Northwest. There, Seattle Seahawks Coach Pete Carroll opens the doors to his practice facility and welcomes them to learn the magic of what has allowed his Seahawks to be so highly successful. From former Microsoft CEO Steve Ballmer to Golden State coach Steve Kerr, these leaders have been studying the way Carroll and his coaching staff communicate with their players.

"You don't see the way they coach often," said Kerr, who went to visit the Seahawks both before and after he led his team to the 2015 NBA

Championship. "There's no yelling and screaming . . . there's teaching. It was liberating to see and had a great influence on me."

Carroll is the master of this discussion on how to engage teammates, especially when things haven't gone right.

"As a leader it is so important to be precise with your language," Carroll said. "We don't like synonyms around here. We say whatever it is it is. We want to keep the message clear for the players so they can own it. It doesn't matter if we have good ideas; they have to be able to utilize them. So we try to be real specific with our language and knowing the power of talk—the positives and the negatives of self talk too. If you're unclear, they have unclear thoughts.

"For instance, when we correct people, we correct them by trying to discipline ourselves as coaches to correct them by telling them what exactly we would like to happen and not what they did wrong," he said. "If a guy releases inside instead of outside on a pattern, we don't say, 'Why did you do that? What were you thinking? We never release like that.' All those words and all those habits of yelling at a guy—we don't have time to do that. We want to put it right into that guy's brain as soon as we can that we always release with our outside foot and grip with our inside arm. We tell them exactly what we desire as quickly as we can instead of wasting airtime with criticism. We want to get to the essence of what is important, and learning is important. But to do that, we as coaches have to be disciplined, because that's not the way most of us were coached earlier in life."

Coach Carroll made the point that he's never met a professional who wanted to make a mistake—drop a pass, miss a tackle, or fumble the ball. So yelling over a mistake accomplishes nothing. But in that moment, a player is at the most important part of the learning curve. Great leaders take advantage of that moment—and a player's willingness to be taught—to speak a different coaching language.

Sue Enquist is a Hall of Fame coach who led her UCLA Bruins women's softball team to eleven national championships as a player and as a coach. She said her career turned as she learned how to have different conversations with her players—especially around conflict.

"The biggest problem with conflict is we both want to be right," Enquist said. "And we're just going to go at each other. As a leader, I had a habit of just showing all of my cards right up front. I don't like you because of this—throwing my cards at you. 'You didn't do this, you didn't do this, you did that—and I didn't come up for air for thirty minutes. Then [the player would] speak for two minutes, and we accomplished nothing. I felt good—but it accomplished nothing.

"The sad part of conflict with a head coach and a player, with a leader and an employee, is you cannot start from an area of neutrality: she's not neutral, and I'm not either. But more times than not, it doesn't matter how far off she is, you have to find out how far off she is, and start from there. Then you can work your way back to neutrality.

"Later in my career I realized I could get to the root of conflict by asking the right questions. I'd start with, 'What are you perceiving is going wrong here?' It's so much more effective. I'd say, 'Now we're not in a good place—you and I. Give me three things right now that you're perceiving.' And then let the conversation start wherever that is. And then you have to work it backwards—meaning—what would it take to get us to a good place? What do I need to do? Put it on me. Learning to flip that script changed my coaching career."

The other advantage of "flipping the script," Enquist said, was that having the player speak first "was like being in a negotiation: you never want to be the first one to throw out a number." She said making that change allowed her to increase the effectiveness of her conversations, especially in conflict situations.

Jack Clark, former head coach of the US national rugby team and current head coach for the University of California Golden Bears rugby team, supercharges his team culture with a secret weapon: praise. Under Clark's tenure, the Golden Bears have won twenty-two national titles, including a dozen in a row from 1991 to 2002 and five consecutive ones from 2004 to 2008. Though Clark's team has amassed incredible success, nothing has been more rewarding for him than discovering what his athletes do best.

Throughout his career, Clark has been on the search for the ultimate motivator for his players. He has used trial and error, anecdotal information from other head coaches, body language, and goal setting, all with minimal results. But Clark found a winning combination when he learned about neuroscience—specifically, positive reinforcement—and how his communication could revolutionize his one-on-one meetings with his athletes.

"What happens to all coaches and managers over time is that they settle into a certain way and keep a routine regarding athlete management," Clark said to me. "But our research into neuroscience helped me to focus on the positive aspects of my team's performance to motivate them."

Clark used this approach to revamp his one-on-one player evaluations, where he would make a point of communicating the strengths of each rugby player to that player in person.

"Whenever one of us is in front of our superiors or coaches, the whole conversation is about what we need to do better, and I have kind of grown out of that," Clark admitted. "I'm not really interested in what people don't do well anymore. Truly, leaders should always put some work plans together to acquire skill in areas wherever there is deficiency, but ultimately you have to build on an approach or blueprint for individuals based on what their strengths are."

Clark says he spends 70 percent of his conversations on the best qualities of his players. This approach has created opportunities for his team to maximize their strengths in a way that completely overwhelms—and overpowers—opponents.

"The moment any of this works right, it forms the majority of your conversations with that player over the course of the year, and you're never in a more intimate relationship with that player than when you are modeling on their strengths," Clark said. "My athletes leave those meetings walking on top of the world.

"There's not a thing we can do better for people than have their superiors know what they do well, which gives people a great sense of satisfaction—better than a raise, starting a job, or a lot of things that you would think would really motivate them."

Oakland University men's basketball head coach Greg Kampe uses *The Wizard of Oz* as inspiration for communicating his "yellow brick road" team philosophy. In the movie—and within the culture of OU basketball—the lead actors find themselves in trouble when they stray too far away from the yellow brick road. So each year Kampe conducts a ceremony in which every incoming freshman receives a yellow brick from the team captains. The bricks, with the team creed printed on the surface, serve as reminders for the players to stay on the right path. The players are encouraged to write personalized messages on their own bricks and to remember that they represent the culture of Oakland University.

"The bricks are a daily reminder to our players that they are warriors, members of a team, and serve Oakland University and its nation of fans—to always place the team first, to never accept defeat or quit, to persevere and thrive on adversity, to be physically harder and mentally stronger than opponents, and to draw on every remaining ounce of strength to protect their teammates and accomplish the mission," Kampe said. "Our players are guardians of the traditions and values of those who carried the bricks before them."

The players carry their bricks through the four years of their educations. Upon graduation, they hand their bricks—and the pressure to continue the tradition—off to the next class of freshmen.

In the 2004–5 NBA playoffs, the Miami Heat—who had added center Shaquille O'Neal before the season began—took the Detroit Pistons to a final and decisive Game 7 in the Eastern Conference finals. The Heat ended up losing the game by a heartbreaking six points. In the off-season, Heat president Pat Riley had made a series of controversial trades and acquisitions, bringing in aging veterans Antoine Walker, Jason Williams, and Gary Payton. Critics felt it was a bad idea to surround rising superstar Dwyane Wade with players who were past their prime, but Riley felt that veterans were exactly what the team needed to reach the next level. But even Wade had doubts.

"Next thing you know, we're welcoming eight new players to training camp shortly after the team pulled off the biggest trade in NBA history, which involved thirteen players and five teams," Wade wrote after the season. "I remember guys thinking, 'We had a great team the year before, so why the change, especially now?' I would be lying if I said that we didn't have doubts, not with the players coming in but about changing what we believed to be an already great team. Early in the season, we were playing .500 ball, so those doubts only grew bigger, not only internally, but also from the media following the team."[1]

After twenty-one games of the 2005–6 regular season, the Heat had an 11–10 record. A major part of the problem was that O'Neal had missed eighteen of those games with a foot injury. However, there was also disharmony on the team because so many players were unhappy with the overwrought coaching style of Stan Van Gundy. The situation got downright chaotic when Van Gundy resigned, citing personal reasons. Riley quickly assumed coaching duties, and though the team played better after that, there were still leadership issues to resolve.

In the middle of the regular season, the Dallas Mavericks embarrassed Miami in a nationally televised game, winning by thirty-six points. Doubts about Riley's leadership resurfaced, and soon thereafter he met with Wade to discuss unifying the team.

In a passionate display of leadership, Riley then met with the rest of the Heat and told them that if they wanted to accomplish their goal of an NBA title, it would take the effort of all fifteen guys on the roster. As the playoffs began, Riley distributed cards emblazoned with the phrase "15

Strong" to each of his players and then demanded their ultimate dedication. The team rallied behind the message and Riley's leadership, and the cards became a permanent fixture in the Heat's locker rooms throughout the playoff run.

The team made significant progress after that. The Heat returned to the Eastern Conference finals against the Detroit Pistons team and won the series 4–2, clinching a berth in the championship round. The 2006 NBA finals series was an epic rematch against the Dallas Mavericks, who quickly took control by winning the first two games.

The situation looked bleak. Only two teams in the history of the NBA had ever returned from a two-game deficit in the finals. It was the ultimate test of the Heat's commitment to the "15 Strong" concept. But the commitment was real.

"Riley understands what's necessary for a team to be truly successful," said Bruce Bowen, a forward who played a year for the Heat before moving on to greatness with the San Antonio Spurs. "He knows what a team can accomplish when it has structure and discipline."

In Game 3, the Heat rallied from a thirteen-point deficit and bested the Mavericks with a game-winning shot from veteran guard Gary Payton. That victory swung momentum into the Heat's favor, and the team went on to win the final four games of the series, capturing its first NBA championship.

The 2006 Heat demonstrated a unique ability to remain focused in moments of adversity, particularly as the series against Dallas unfolded. Even the contrast of leadership styles between the Heat and the Mavericks was very telling. With each loss, Mavericks team owner Mark Cuban would complain to referees or throw a tantrum on the sidelines. Furthermore, because Cuban sat directly behind the team bench, many Dallas players fed off of the negativity from Cuban and lost their cool during the series. The Heat, by contrast, handled the series with the composure of a Great Team; they demonstrated a collective purpose and energy that endured challenge after challenge. As a team they were completely unified in the goal of winning an NBA championship.

During the locker-room celebration, Riley revealed to the media the secret weapon behind his team's success: a container filled with thousands of laminated pieces of card stock with the phrase "15 Strong" printed on each one. The phrase had changed the dynamic of the Heat's season and helped turn the tide of the NBA finals.

For all of these teams, speaking a different language—using inspiring words, asking better questions, finding unique ways to draw others in—has been integral to their success.

AND FOR THE TRULY GREAT TEAMS IN BUSINESS

Great Teams create cultures with solid foundations in positive reinforcement. Walt Disney World and Disneyland acknowledges superstar employees—which the company refers to as "Cast Members"—on the spot with its Guest Service Fanatic cards. Whenever Disney management (or any fellow employee) notices a Cast Member truly living and expressing the company's service values of safety, courtesy, show, and efficiency,[2] the actions of the employee are recognized on the spot by handing out the cards. Card recipients are eligible for drawings, and copies of the cards are kept in the recipients' personnel files.[3]

"We encourage all Cast Members to be leaders in their area," wrote Jeff James, vice president and general manager of the Disney Institute, in a blog for the company. "We believe that a leader is someone who makes an impact regardless of his or her title. To implement change, you must reward and recognize individuals when they do something right."[4]

The cards have been beneficial to Disney because 1) leaders are expected to be on alert for employees who are living the values and 2) Cast Members are recognized for doing their jobs well and reinforcing culture. Additionally, the cards serve as fantastic leadership indicators when the company is seeking dedicated employees for promotions.

It's always easier for team leaders to criticize performance, but

Great Teams create cultures that have solid foundations in positive reinforcement.

Great Teams see constructive criticism as opportunities to reinforce culture. Starbucks prides itself on humble beginnings; however, the company suffered a stretch where it was having difficulty retaining this aspect of its culture as it grew into an industry titan. It struggled even more in 2008, as the US economy wobbled. For some during that troubled time, Starbucks became the symbol of excess and rampant consumerism.

The strains of business and the leadership squabbles prompted chairman Howard Schultz to return to the company as CEO after an eight-year hiatus. Once he reinvested himself in company operations, Schultz was not pleased to find differing perceptions of Starbucks among its huge employee pool. He thought that the stores were losing sight of what made the company great.

"When I returned in January 2008, things were actually worse than I'd thought," Schultz said in an interview with the *Harvard Business Review*. "The decisions we had to make were very difficult, but first there had to be a time when we stood up in front of the entire company as leaders and made almost a confession—that the leadership had failed the 180,000 Starbucks people and their families."[5]

Instead of berating Starbucks managers for not reinforcing the brand's image among employees, however, Schultz sought to remedy the issue with additional training. On February 26, 2008, the organization closed all the stores in North America and took a three-hour "learning break" so that every employee could be reimmersed in the practices of making an ideal cup of coffee.

"We were asking our people to do too much, to chase after too many new ideas that took us away from our core business, so we pulled the plug on lots of things and focused on the ones that were most important," Schultz said.[6]

With the training, employees relearned best practices, and managers realized they could empower subordinates to coach other employees. The session was incredibly beneficial for the employees, as it demonstrated the pride Starbucks took in its people, the company, and the brand—and its willingness to invest in all three.

GREAT TAKEAWAYS

Communication that inspires, motivates, and encourages is one of the most important steps in achieving greatness. Through the good and bad, articulating praise and criticism in positive ways is essential to the success of the team. When you speak the language of a Great Team, you communicate constructive feedback that penetrates even the most unwilling ears—and keeps people motivated long after the feedback has been received.

So how can you learn to speak this different language? Consider these language lessons:

1. Be an example for others to follow. Leaders must be living examples of the change they wish to see in their teams. If your position includes managing others, then you must understand how to communicate effectively. Leaders who clearly explain goals and expectations set models for their organizations to follow. They also recognize areas within their own communication styles that need improvement.

2. Ask the right questions. Leaders who wish to empower their teams begin by asking the right questions. This means, of course, that you need to listen first. And when something goes wrong, reframing your words can have a tremendous value in how an employee receives correction. Instead of asking, "Why do you keep messing up?" be a leader who says, "What can we do to help you meet your next deadline?" or "How can we make your job more manageable?"

3. Use effective verbal praise. Anyone can spend hours discussing negatives and weaknesses, but a Great Team uses precious time to identify the strengths of its team members and to focus on improving those strengths. Words of affirmation are powerful because they highlight a positive characteristic of another person in a clear and definite manner. When leaders verbally celebrate an employee's accomplishment or favorable behavior, those leaders are also sending a message to other employees, challenging them to emulate the same behaviors. Thus, verbal praise subtly reinforces culture. As Jack Clark demonstrated with his rugby players, words of praise can be highly beneficial to the forward momentum of a team.

4. Affirm character. Quite often, the most admirable character traits are overlooked by members of a professional team. Sure, many of us may seek to cultivate traits such as determination, humility, honesty, patience, and integrity in ourselves. But ask yourself, "Have I expressed gratitude to *others* who possess these characteristics?" Like those who hand out Guest Service Fanatic Cards at Walt Disney World, Great Team leaders observe their teams, note strong examples of character, and celebrate them accordingly, then use the process as research for future success. Leaders should practice verbalizing affirmations so that when the opportunity comes, they can praise team members in a meaningful and effective way.

5. Know how and where to affirm. Great Teams use communication like game plans—strategically and creatively. Communication should be personal, specific, and within an appropriate context. Private conversations between leaders and employees can deepen rapport and build trust. Public affirmations, on the other hand, set a standard of expectancy and aspiration. Rewarding employees in front of others can also inspire the entire team to strive for similar results.

Great Teams

Language matters. A shift in communication can be an important cornerstone in a company's culture. Genuine affirmations, along with constructive feedback, can positively change the dynamic of an organization. Additionally, verbal praise can directly impact the sense of "why" or deeper purpose for everyone on the team. And acknowledging character can help ensure that nobody strays far from the intended course.

The Great Teams see the value of speaking a different language, setting them apart from competitors.

CHAPTER 16

GREAT TEAMS AVOID THE PITFALLS OF SUCCESS

They seek to sustain success by resisting complacency and distractions.

Even a Great Team can be its own worst enemy, especially once it *becomes* a Great Team. Whether they raise a championship banner or rise to the top of their industry, even the best teams can be defeated by complacency—they spend too much time sleeping in their trophy rooms—or an inability to start fresh as a new season begins.

The sports and business greats know that as difficult as winning is, winning repeatedly is more challenging by a factor of ten. Even after defeating all competitors, some organizations are truly unprepared for victory. A team that does not know how to navigate success will ultimately be thrown off track in its attempts to succeed further. The Great Teams maintain success by not falling victim to the pitfalls of human nature; they overcome common temptations, resist complacency, and nurture a culture that wins consistently. Winners capitalize on new opportunities, adjust game plans, and do not settle for what worked last season or year.

The great John Wooden, whom I have mentioned several times in this book, often said, "Winning takes talent; to repeat takes character."[1] It also takes avoiding the four pitfalls that tend to work against a team's remaining at the top:

- The bull's-eye effect
- Complacency
- Fear of breaking the streak
- Staff turnover

GREAT TEAMS IN SPORTS

Industry leaders or defending champions will always be targets for opportunistic competitors. In such cases, a team must go the extra mile to remain on top and continue to meet newly raised expectations. The bull's-eye effect is a natural symptom of success; any team that has reached the top automatically becomes the giant everyone else wants to slay. The chance to dethrone a champion is an incredible motivator for even the lowest-performing teams, and a champion should never underestimate a competitor's efforts.

Complacency is perhaps the most common pitfall. A hard-fought victory or successful season can make even the most dedicated organizations drop their guards or spend just a little too much time patting themselves on their collective backs. Overcelebration can easily consume the mood of an entire organization, stifle improvement efforts, rot work ethic, and create laziness. The glow of victory makes the pain and sacrifice of a championship easy to forget; however, Great Teams reject the sense of entitlement that comes after an epic win or championship. To win continuously, a team has to challenge the false belief that what's been accomplished will naturally happen again.

University of Florida head softball coach Tim Walton understands the challenge. After winning the 2014 NCAA national championship—while basking in the warmth of victory—Walton was unsure of how to proceed with his team.

He struggled with delivering a new message of hard work to his talented squad in the midst of their celebrations. So to move forward, he returned to the glue that held his team together—culture and values. He made very clear to his players the expectations that came from winning a national championship. Not only would they enter the preseason ranked number one, but they'd have to battle overconfidence.

"The reality was that the public was going to expect great things from us," Walton shared with me in an interview. "I told my players that the only way we would win another championship was for us to develop the ability to be a lunch-pail team. We need to be workers."

Walton meant this quite literally. He installed a time clock in the Lady Gator's practice facility to drive home this blue-collar approach, and he presented each player with an old-fashioned metal lunch pail.

"Every day when our girls arrived, they'd punch into the time clock and take their ticket," Walton said. "This was a symbolic way of saying that nothing else matters beyond this point, so check your baggage at the door because you are here to work."

Each week Walton and his staff placed bouncy balls and index cards with motivational definitions into each player's lunch pail to add value not only to her week but to her season as well.

"The ball represented resiliency," he explained to me. "Once bounced, it doesn't stay on the ground very long. The ball doesn't stay *down*. I told my players that failure is unavoidable, but they should always be like the ball and have the ability to bounce back."

Scribbled on the front of each index card was a word, with the definition of that word on the back. (*Unselfishness*, for instance, was defined as "putting the team first.") These cards helped the Lady Gators rally around a common team-first language to reinforce their hardworking culture.

Walton's motivation theme caught on fast. Players brought their lunch pails to home and away games, and they regularly shouted their index-card messages when cheering for teammates—even teammates who made mistakes.

"How you respond to a mistake is more important than the mistake itself," Walton said. "Teaching our players how to respond to their own personal failures and to their teammate's failures was the reinforcement of character components that helped us move in a positive direction."

Walton's leadership in this situation is fascinating because he and his team rejected the typical championship letdown that most teams face after a winning season. Repeat championships in both the sports and business worlds are rare because most teams fail to create new motivations or innovations. By stressing the universal value of hard work, Walton and his Lady Gators were able to remove themselves from their previously successful season and start fresh. Ultimately, these values brought the Lady Gators—and their lunch pails—back to the playoffs in Oklahoma City, where they won their second consecutive national championship in 2015.

University of Alabama head football coach Nick Saban is one of the greatest coaches in college football's modern era. His record in the ultra-competitive Southeastern Conference has been impeccable. He's won four national championships over an eight-year span—first at LSU and then at Alabama—and he led the Crimson Tide to back-to-back national titles in 2011 and 2012.

When it comes to winning consistently, Saban understands that success and satisfaction repel like the two negative ends of batteries. In 2003, his LSU Tigers handily defeated the Georgia Bulldogs 34–13 in the SEC championship game, clinching a chance to play for the national title. And less than an hour after winning that SEC title—while the rest of the LSU players and coaching staff were still celebrating the victory—Saban met with his agent, Jimmy Sexton. Sexton was shocked by how anxious and dour Saban looked while everyone else joined in the jubilation.

"What's wrong?" Sexton asked.

"I hate all this," Saban admitted. "It's going to put me behind in recruiting."

In recounting the story to me, Sexton simply shook his head. "That's just how he's built."

Saban's LSU Tigers went on to win the national championship that year, but it was not the last time he would display discomfort in the face of success. Throughout his coaching career, the slightest sense of complacency was almost frightening to him. All that mattered was the next challenge and the next opportunity to win.

Saban understood the role that past success plays in undermining a Great Team's shot at continuing that success. Victory brings trophies and praise, but it also brings challenges and obstacles that are harder to identify because they are not dipped in gold or handed out as bonus checks. Complacency sabotages a team's chances to win long before the next game is ever played.

When a team is dominant, it is easy to believe the hype. These pitfalls are the hidden traps that prevent teams from developing a tradition of winning consistently.

MORE FROM THE GREAT TEAMS IN SPORTS

With six undefeated seasons and eleven championship wins under his belt, University of Connecticut women's basketball coach Geno Auriemma proves that a resilient culture is capable of navigating the pitfalls of success. But even with all of their accomplishments, the Lady Huskies players live constantly with the fear of not meeting expectations. This fear can easily plague teams that have achieved a stretch of tremendous success. Ironically, the fear of underperforming can actually *create* an underperforming team—especially if its members play "not to lose" instead of to win.

To combat this tendency, Coach Auriemma runs incredibly demanding practices that push his players past their comfort zones; for example, he might match a five-player team against seven opponents. As they push their way through these intense sessions, the pressure to perform becomes influenced by team voices—such as Coach Auriemma's—instead of the outside pressure to keep the win streak alive.

Additionally, Coach Auriemma talks openly with his players about his expectations and challenges them in positive ways—often through the media—to improve their game and develop new skills. Prior to the team's 2009 NCAA title game against Louisville, whom UConn had defeated twice during the regular season, Auriemma told reporters, "I don't know if what we did to them in the first game had any effect on the second game. And what we did to them in the second game, I don't know that it has any effect on today. These are different environments, different days, and different attitudes among the players. I mean, there's no disputing the fact that we won by a lot both times. But I don't know what that gets you. You still have to go out and make the shots and stop them."

The Lady Huskies realized they weren't playing against just an overmatched opponent—they were playing against the expectations of their head coach. The message resonated, and UConn crushed Louisville for a third time to take the 2009 NCAA title.

Turnover can cripple any successful team. However, staff stability is a factor that kept head coach Bobby Bowden's Florida State University football teams consistently dominant. The program's first national championship in 1993 was the culmination of a stable core of assistant coaches who all bought into Bowden's coaching methods. "One of the things that happens when you win," Bowden told me, "is that everyone tries to hire your staff. They think that if they can just grab one of your guys that they'll get results. That's tempting to the coaches, because they're often waving bigger money and prestige. Our good fortune was that our guys stayed and stayed together for so long."

The consistency on the sidelines boosted team success; Coach Bowden's teams spent fourteen straight years winning at least ten games per season and finishing in the top five of the Associated Press's top-25 national rankings. In the 1990s alone, FSU lost just 13 times and won 109 games—the most victories in NCAA history by any team during any decade.

"You win and win and win, and then pressure continues to build," Bowden shared with me. "But I know one thing: it's easier to get to the top than it is to stay there."

Bowden—now retired and in the College Football Hall of Fame with 377 career wins—will be the first to admit that his success during the FSU dynasty years was a direct result of keeping his talented coaching staff intact. He credits giving his coaches tough responsibilities that not only motivated and empowered them, but also "strengthen[ed] loyalty to the team's continued success" instead of individual pursuits. He referred to this strategy as "getting the right coaches and then getting out of their way."

AND FOR THE TRULY GREAT TEAMS IN BUSINESS

The Great Teams are led by culturally intelligent leaders. These individuals understand the impact that a strong workplace culture can have on goal completion and focus-driven work. And a culturally perceptive team can be especially valuable during challenging times. In a survey by global management consulting firm Bain & Company, 91 percent of the top twelve hundred senior executives of the world's highest-performing companies reported that culture is an important component of success— and sustenance. Another Bain study found that 81 percent of corporate executives agreed that an organization without a winning culture will never surpass mediocrity.[2]

Entrepreneur Glenn Llopis writes that "cultural intelligence exists when a company trusts itself enough to live the promise of its culture in how its brands communicate with its audience and consistently delivers on that promise."[3] Winning organizations sustain success by accommodating the evolving needs of the marketplace while simultaneously remaining true to the "cultural promise" they make to consumers.

The most successful brands of our time—such as Nike, McDonald's, Google, and Apple—tend to transcend the marketplace, ultimately becoming something much greater than a brand: a *meaning*. A brand becomes symbolic by keeping cultural promises in an ever-changing society; its relevance is embedded in its desire to remain significant. Likewise, risk-taking organizations outperform companies that play it safe during periods of change. These teams seek and create new possibilities with an innovative spirit.

Southwest Airlines, the world's largest low-cost airline, leads a competitive marketplace by remaining true to its number one value: organizational culture. The organization ranks its employees first, customers second, and shareholders third.[4] This unorthodox ranking ensures that Southwest always knows who drives the company and to whom they are in service. And it has led the company to repeated success.

CEO Gary Kelly, who has worked for Southwest since 1986, learned these lessons from Carl Icahn, former owner of Trans World Airlines (TWA). The two met in 1988 at a conference, when Southwest was still a fledgling airline with no more than sixty planes. At the time, Icahn sat tall on TWA's industry dominance. As keynote speaker at the conference, he described the challenges of leading a dominant airline. As part of his comments on dealing with labor unions, Icahn made a tongue-in-cheek reference to tiny Southwest that earned several laughs from the industry crowd.

Clearly, Icahn did not see Southwest as a competitor at the time. But Kelly saw himself as a competitor, and he has never forgotten Icahn's dismissive attitude. "The lesson to me was that no matter how big you are, you need to remain humble," he said to me in an interview. "It pays to be hungry, and you should never lose your competitive edge, because there is always somebody out there trying to knock you off."

Today, TWA is forgotten and Southwest is America's favorite airline, with more than thirty-eight hundred flights a day to ninety-seven destinations in forty-one states and, as of 2015, seven other countries. In 2013, Southwest was ranked number one in customer satisfaction by the US Department of Transportation.[5] And yet the airline places employee happiness above customer satisfaction. "We believe that if we treat our employees right, they will treat our customers right, and in turn that results in increased business and profits that make everyone happy," the airline explained in a Southwest blog post about its company culture.[6]

Southwest regularly competes with a number of smaller carriers in a hunt for the airline's business. In light of this competition, Kelly tries to reinforce the spirit of humility throughout his entire organization. "We have to remain as humble as we were in the 1980s because in the next thirty years, we may find ourselves facing a more formidable competitor," he said. "Those that are modest today could be tomorrow's dominant carrier if we are not careful."

In order to sustain success in a competitive field, Kelly and his culturally intelligent team have paid special attention to not only their field of competitors, but society as a whole. Through this extensive study, Southwest has developed into a company known for its diversity, customer service, affordability, fun, and respect. By focusing on culture building, Southwest has maintained a dominant lead over direct competitors United Airlines, Delta, JetBlue, and Spirit.

"We make a tremendous effort to understand who we are, what we want to be, and the gaps that we might have in our performance," Kelly said. "We have a constant awareness of what is going on around us and what our competitors are doing and how we compare to them. We try to find out what our customers are saying and evaluate if we are living up to their expectations."

Culture plays a pivotal role in Kelly's organization, and his employees' happiness is a constant, strategic point that can be connected to great customer service. By maintaining a fun, open environment, Southwest reminds its employees to always enjoy their work. This approach upgrades a trip on Southwest from a flight to an experience—which ultimately translates into customer-pleasing performance.

"Every company has a culture, and every group has a culture. It is just whether you want the culture to be good or bad," Kelly said. "In our case, we recognize the value of people, and we invest in those relationships and they are genuine. And I think that creates a very powerful team within a family-like environment."

Southwest's investment in its employees takes many forms, including celebrations, features in company newsletters, and videos that circulate the Southwest intranet and staff meetings. Since company marketing materials often showcase individual employees, Southwest staff reap the benefits of public recognition. It's not unusual for customers to recognize Southwest's "celebrity" employees when taking a flight.

Southwest Airlines is a Great Team because its culture, its relentless pursuit of customer satisfaction, and its investment in its employees consistently place it leagues ahead of the competition. "Resiliency is important in business, especially in our industry," Kelly said. "But when people think of our culture, they will see an organization that cares for others. So the culture helps define what is important, it helps confirm what is important to our purpose."

GREAT TAKEAWAYS

The Great Teams avoid the common pitfalls of success by defying human nature. Like Saban at Alabama, consistently dominant teams realize that the most common reaction to any success is satisfaction. Overcelebration breeds complacency, and many championship teams fail to repeat due to a lack of focus after an epic win.

For a team desiring to avoid a championship hangover, leaders should limit the time focused on celebrating victories—even as the championship banners are being raised. It's never too early for a team to discuss the temptations of victory and new goals worth fighting for.

The teams that sustain success make daily commitments to improve themselves and the company rather than rest on their laurels. Their leaders are culturally intelligent, and they restlessly search to find inspiration in the opportunities of tomorrow. They understand that what brought success won't keep it.

In the pursuit of greatness, these teams aren't afraid to put their streak on the line when chasing after a new challenge. They always play to win instead of "not to lose."

Successful teams should ask themselves, "How do we respond after a record year? In what ways can we defy the natural human tendency to coast?" Leaders should set aside time after an epic win to discuss new ventures, strategies, and improvements while the previous season or quarter is still fresh in everyone's minds. This is the time to look deep within and also to examine the marketplace—to spot needs waiting to be filled and come up with unique ways to meet those needs.

Repeat champions and industry leaders know how to handle the bull's-eye effect. These winners stay aware of the targets on their backs and revel in the idea that competitors want nothing more than to take them down. As Southwest Airlines demonstrated with TWA, hungry competitors dethrone corporate giants all the time. But the Great Teams thrive in the midst of competition, leverage their platforms into new spheres of influence, and use the reality of the bull's-eye effect as motivation to remain innovative.

How do you handle the thought of failure? If you are currently sitting on a winning streak, do you merely play "not to lose" instead of to win? Does your team share this same mind-set? The greatest champions of our time expect to win. Why shouldn't your team?

For a Great Team, repeat success is often a byproduct of a high-performing culture. Maintaining championship or industry-leading momentum requires experienced leadership, cultural drivers, and clear communication of the end goal and how to get there. Team members must be connected to the new direction of an organization; people want to feel excited about the future and the potential of progress. Progressive leaders understand these truths and connect their teams to a culture that motivates, challenges, and empowers them to start and to keep winning. The captains of industry don't stew in failure and defeat but instead are forward thinking, doggedly chasing after the next great opportunity.

Always strive to remember the pitfalls of success—and don't let them derail your Great Team!

APPENDIX

Great Takeaways from Business and Sports Leaders

GANON BAKER

Basketball personal training entrepreneur; former Division I collegiate coach

Lead through repetition and inspiration. This is "the best way to develop young talent." "Motivation is short, but inspiration lasts a lifetime."

Greatness comes from enthusiasm for the game. "Seeing passion from players always gives a coach confidence," Baker said. "Great winners always have a passion in what they do."

COLONEL BERNIE BANKS

Head of Department of Behavioral Sciences and Leadership and former program director for Eisenhower Leader Development Program, United States Military Academy, West Point

Create an action plan. "Leadership lessons can help someone grow if they take advice and tailor it specifically to their own ideas and goals," Banks said. Additionally, Banks believes that you need to create a game plan based on advice you hear. Specifically, "How do we foster the realization lesson but do it in a way that is authentic to our own organization?"

Don't fight your last war. "You don't train for your next opponent by preparing the same way that you did when facing your previous opponent," Banks said. "You don't know what your next opponent is going to bring to the table, so you have to be able to train broadly."

BOBBY BOWDEN

Two-time national champion and former head
coach of Florida State University football

Think "win." When Coach Bowden arrived at FSU, the program's mind-set toward winning was indifferent. Coach Bowden's top priority as a new coach was to change that mind-set to one where winning was the ultimate goal.

Trust your staff. "I hired coaches whom I trusted to run certain parts of the program, and I trusted them to handle the responsibility without constant supervision," Bowden said. Avoiding micromanagement improved staff morale and allowed Coach Bowden to focus on running an entire program.

BRUCE BOWEN

Three-time NBA champion with the San Antonio Spurs

It's not just about a game. "Great competitors focus on daily improvement, with the mind-set to win each and every day," Bowen said.

Challenges are learning opportunities. Bowen believes that challenging situations can be integral to creating growth, learning, and accountability. Those who persevere through these circumstances are more experienced and knowledgeable when they encounter future obstacles.

Discipline makes the difference. "Great teams have to be talented, but they also have to be disciplined," Bowen said. "Discipline is the difference between selfish play by star players and team-oriented basketball."

Preparation shows in critical moments. "In tense situations, we are creatures of habit," Bowen said. "When a game gets into crunch time, players lean on their most comfortable moves and shots." So it's especially important that those are the right moves, *made* comfortable by practice and preparation.

AJA BROWN

Mayor of Compton, California

Every leader needs vision. "I think every leader must have a heart of service," said Brown.

Being a leader means cultivating leadership in others. "In order to be an effective leader, you have to mobilize other leaders around you. It's critical to be able to see things in other people that sometimes they don't see in themselves. . . . As long as you can cultivate great leaders around you, you can increase your capacity and be more effective."

Leaders create team buy-in by caring. "Regardless of what the mission is, we are still humans, and we have needs to be addressed," said Brown. "An effective leader is able to reach people in their natural environment and extract their experiences and knowledge about the issues that impact them. By this, you can show that you care about people not just from words, but by spending time and making sure they have the resources that they need."

DALE BROWN

Former head coach of Louisiana State University men's basketball

Your players need you to defend them. "There's an old saying that 'they don't care how much you know until they know how much you care.' That was a driving force in the relationship I wanted to have with my players. There is no way they could leave our program without knowing how much I cared for them—not just as players but as people," Brown said.

Make sure everyone knows how you value them. "God doesn't make any junk. My job as a leader is to remind others of that— and to remember it myself. Being a coach is tough work with lots of people who feel free to share their opinions about you."

JIM CALHOUN
Former head coach of University of Connecticut men's basketball (1986–2012); three-time NCAA champion

Celebrate daily victories. "I believe in winning the day and looking for small victories for my players, whether a great play in practice, a passing grade on an exam, or a personal best in the weight room," Calhoun said. "I used these opportunities to reinforce behavior that was consistent with the culture I wanted to build." It was no coincidence that many of the daily victories he celebrated with his players were related to academics. This focus represented an important team culture shift in his early days at UConn.

Take pride in your work ethic. Calhoun understood the importance of passion and motivation. "During practice, I would remind my players of how hard the other Great Teams were working at that moment, because I wanted my players to feel pride in their work ethic," he said.

JOHN CALIPARI
Head coach of University of Kentucky men's basketball; 2012 national champion

Students provide guidance to other students. Calipari has a structure in place for older students to advise incoming freshmen about life as a student-athlete. He believes in making the program student oriented, and he wants the athletes to understand that the program's design gives them the tools to succeed and accomplish their goals on and off the court.

Be honest about challenges, and don't use promises as a recruiting tool. When recruiting players to Kentucky, Calipari is up front about the challenge they are facing. He does not promise playing time, shots, or a game plan tailored to the incoming players. "Promising something, such as playing time, is setting up for disappointment and a breakdown of trust," said Calipari.

Offer servant leadership. This is Calipari's main principle at Kentucky. The primary role of a leader on the team is to serve the players around him. Calipari extends this principle to his staff as well. He sees himself as a servant leader to his staff and encourages his staff to act as servant leaders to each other, providing support and encouragement and speaking well of them: "Whenever you are speaking about one of the assistants, go and be his PR machine. So if anybody asks me about any of you, I'm your PR machine. You are my PR machine. Each of you are each other's PR machine."

PETE CARROLL

Head coach and executive vice president of the Seattle Seahawks; former head coach of New England Patriots and University of Southern California football; won both the Super Bowl and the college national championship

Collaborate for love of the sport. Carroll regularly meets with like-minded coaches such as Anson Dorrance of the University of North Carolina to trade best practices on communicating a sense of winning and purpose with a team. He pursues this collaborative connection for many reasons, but simple love of the sport is foremost. Carroll loves "being involved in the competition," and he wants other coaches to know "the time that they spend with their players can be so valuable and so fruitful in so many ways." He "just feels connected to answering their questions and sharing whatever it is in an attempt to shed some light."

The most crucial aspect is authenticity and knowing yourself. Carroll strongly believes that authenticity and truth are at the backbone of being successful and powerful. He wants his athletes to be able "to discover what is inside themselves and to realize how crucial it is to know themselves." Carroll wants the coaches with whom he meets to realize players "have to figure out who they are" so that they can reach the core of what is most important.

JACK CLARK

Former head coach of US national rugby team; head coach of University of California men's rugby; twenty-two-time national champion

Be grateful for everything and entitled to nothing. This is a phrase Clark uses with his team to explain their culture. "We believe in important values that create our system where we can process everything that happens on and off the field," Clark said. "We believe in things like selflessness. I'm going to talk about performance improvement, I'm going to talk about merit, I'm going to talk about toughness, and I'm going to talk about leadership. These values are broad enough that they include most things that will happen to a teammate, and they don't contradict each other."

Overcome adversity. Clark knows the hardest time to hang on to cultural values is when the team is going through adversity. "You know when you have sixty-five boys on the team, someone is going to . . . have some real things happening in their life," Clark said. "I mean, it's easy to keep your values chugging along, and everybody is contributing to them when things are going well. It's when things go pear-shaped that you need to keep everyone aware of your values."

JERRY COLANGELO

Chairman of USA Basketball; former chairman of basketball operations for Philadelphia 76ers; chairman of Naismith Memorial Basketball Hall of Fame

Culture can't be changed by committee. "To have success at changing a culture, you need to have a singular vision," Colangelo said. "Culture by committee" is an idea that may seem ideal but is set up for failure from the beginning. Great cultures have a strong vision, and that vision comes from the top.

Team players make all the difference. When building his Olympic teams, Colangelo looks for an all-star team, not a team of all stars. "How your team complements each other is just as important as their individual skill sets," he said.

Look for enthusiastic leadership. Colangelo knew Coach Mike Krzyzewski was a proven winner and leader, and he showed the kind of enthusiasm that could be used in building a Great Team. "The most important trait that I saw from Coach K was his optimism in rebuilding an Olympic-gold team," Colangelo said.

BARRY COLLIER

Vice president and director of athletics at Butler University

Use key goals to bond players and staff. Collier encourages bonding through promoting team goals. "The goals for the team, whether long term or short term, are explained to the entire organization—even visiting recruits—to encourage buy-in," Collier said.

A team is like a tree. "When older players leave, a core of younger players and coaches remain to form new branches and leaves, but the culture forms the base and trunk," Collier said. "As players and assistants come and go, the values must remain the same. Those leaders are your base and trunk."

Player buy-in is important. At Butler the players must own the program. Collier believes in asking his players to take responsibility for themselves and each other. "The trust shown by the players and the ownership they feel for the program helps develop them into leaders," Collier said.

A memorable motto can join past, present, and future. "The Butler Way motto is a bridge between the past success of the school and the future success for which the athletes are preparing," Collier said. "It teaches the players to play to their strengths today and improve [their] weaknesses for tomorrow. The Butler Way demands commitment, denies selfishness, accepts reality, but seeks improvement every day, putting the team above self."

TOM CREAN

Head coach of Indiana University men's basketball

There's no such thing as too much communication. "When communication breaks down, mistrust and bad attitudes begin to develop," said Crean. "I remain in constant communication with my players and staff to ensure they are all on the same page."

Chemistry is not just for the players. "Chemistry extends to the entire organization, and we work to promote chemistry between the coaches, players, and the entire organization."

Adversity can be your friend. "A loss or defeat can be the best thing that ever happened to you and your team, simply because it exposes your weakness and shows you what you need to develop," Crean said. "If you see a defeat as an opportunity to learn something, adversity is a great teacher. Through this, all challenges can be overcome by embracing resolve, caring, and building team unity."

RANDY CROSS

Broadcaster and sports analyst; three-time Super Bowl
champion as San Francisco 49ers offensive lineman

Have a plan for meetings. Each 49er knew his role in the huddle, and as a result the huddles were more efficient. "Great teams know how to listen in a meeting and understand when feedback is required," Cross said.

Accountability is very important. "Hold the team, and yourself, accountable to meeting plans," Cross said. "Every huddle follows the same procedure, whether in practice or a game."

COMMANDER RORKE DENVER

Former US Navy SEAL and director of SEAL training
programs; author, motivational speaker, and actor

Leaders must be people of character and value equality. Denver values judgment, even though it is not as easily quantifiable as other things. Leaders need "a moral and ethical compass to have the ability to make decisions that are required for an organization to flourish," Denver said.

Leaders set the pace. "The best leaders can transform a culture," Denver said. "They know how to promote a good operating environment for people to thrive. Efficient leaders are able to see the immediate needs and deficiencies of a culture, make adjustments, and create positive results. This also works in reverse—the worst leaders can bring down a high-performing, positive culture by being unable to see adjustments that need to be made."

Negative team cultures can be clearly identified. "'Me' cultures, or places where employees or team members are constantly looking out for themselves, are indicators of a bad culture," Denver said. "Additionally, places that are stepping stones for employees in order to accomplish a better position or some level of credit are also ineffective cultures. However, organizations where everyone buys in to the company vision have high-performing cultures."

BILL DEWITT JR.

Managing partner and chairman of the St. Louis Cardinals

Use tradition to keep the organization on the same page. "The Cardinal Way is defined as excellence throughout the organization," DeWitt said. "This motto keeps the entire organization on the same page concerning the team's goals and objectives. This tradition is a great responsibility."

Take advantage of the rules. When the MLB implemented a new collective bargaining agreement, DeWitt and the Cardinals shifted their team-building strategy away from free agent signings—an admittedly short-term strategy—to building a solid minor-league foundation by investing in improving facilities and training for their minor leaguers.

BILLY DONOVAN JR.

Head coach of the Oklahoma City Thunder; former head coach of University of Florida men's basketball; two-time NCAA champion

Manage your distractions. "The first time we won our championship, we were unranked, so there was no pressure or expectation," Donovan said. "The second season we won, we were the preseason number-one team, so there was pressure on us to repeat. When your team is that good, the media really puts you under a microscope, and even when you win it's like you didn't play perfectly enough. What I did was [make] a list of all possible distractions, and I went over them with the team and [discussed] how to handle them."

Enjoy the ride. Donovan also thought it was important to not let anyone take the fun out of the journey. "One of the things that happens when your team comes back is that they're put under the microscope. And the fun gets taken out of it because you just went on this unbelievable ride and took everyone by storm the year before. I thought it was important to celebrate and enjoy it because we're in charge of our goal, and that's to come out and win the game. Yes, we didn't play perfectly, but we still won, so let's celebrate and enjoy it."

Don't let your ego take over. Donovan cited a great example in his star center, Joakim Noah, who would go on to play for the Chicago Bulls. "The first year Noah did great; he was the tournament MVP," Donovan said. "But the second year he had two people guarding him instead of just one. Instead of getting frustrated and breaking down, though, he realized that this was opening up opportunities for other players, and he was okay with that. That was really one of the most unselfish acts by a player I've seen."

ANSON DORRANCE

Head coach of University of North Carolina women's soccer; winner of twenty-one NCAA championships

Create and reinforce a principle-centered culture. Anson Dorrance requires his team to memorize the core values of the program. Each value (toughness, discipline, focus, relentlessness, resilience, positivity, class, caring, nobility, selflessness, galvanizing, gratitude) has a definition, and the players are required to learn three per year. "I believe in a principle-centered culture," he said.

Core values should drive evaluations. Every year, Dorrance has his players evaluate their teammates according to the core values. He then meets with each player and goes over how she is perceived by the team.

Measure everything. "My practices are called the 'competitive cauldron' because of my focus on competition and punishing pace,"

Dorrance said. He charts every measurable statistic in practice and ranks the players accordingly. These rankings are posted clearly for the entire team to see as motivation for his players to improve.

KEVIN EASTMAN

Vice president of basketball operations for the Los Angeles Clippers; former assistant coach of the Clippers and the Boston Celtics

Embrace history. While at the Celtics, Eastman and head coach Doc Rivers put an emphasis on the history of the NBA's most storied franchise. Eastman brought in former players to speak to the team about the importance of being a Celtic and the traits needed to be a winning team.

Strong cultures can make transitions seamless. A strong culture, defined as the shared values of the team, will ease the transition of a new member. "A shared culture will quickly show the new team member how he is expected to act," Eastman said.

Strong cultures have standards. These principles are daily reminders of what is important for the team. "Personal agendas are not tolerated within the standards of a strong organization," Eastman said, "because you can't win as a team" when members put themselves first.

Inspiration is different from motivation. "Motivation exists in the short term and is temporary performance," Eastman said. "Inspiration is about the long term and getting the team to believe and buy in to your vision." When coaching the Celtics, Eastman and Rivers met with the players every season to discuss their inspiration for the team.

Coaching and leadership are the same thing in the sports and business worlds. The same principles are used in building a division or a team. "Ultimately, in both sports and business, principles point to results: Who won? Why did they win? What did they do right? What enhancements did they make to win?"

P. J. FLECK

Head coach of Western Michigan University football

Don't be afraid to change. Coach Fleck believes that an organization cannot improve unless change takes place. At WMU he has developed a culture that embraces change on a daily basis. He says that team culture must coincide with organizational transformation so that it can build upon something refreshing and new.

All about perspective. Coach Fleck thinks that a fully rounded coach must have both the player and coaching perspective in order to truly understand both roles. In his view, success lies between connecting the player experience with the job of coaching—something that many organizations fail to do.

Everyone is a leader to somebody, so everyone needs to be a leader. Coach Fleck, his staff, and several WMU football players meet every Thursday for a council on leadership development. Fleck uses the councils to encourage the weakest leaders of his team to improve by performing skits, sharing motivational readings, and providing inspirational stories. "We don't want followers on our program, because everybody influences somebody at some point and that makes you a leader," Fleck said.

WILLIE GAULT

Former wide receiver for the Chicago Bears (1983–87) and the
Los Angeles Raiders (1988–93); Super Bowl champion

Dysfunction isn't an excuse for failure. The 1985 Chicago Bears were set up for failure, with two coaches continuously at odds with one another. But in the course of recording the "Super Bowl Shuffle," a groundbreaking rap song and video that became a hit on the charts, the team members agreed that they had to band together and not let the disagreements and confrontations by their coaches affect their focus.

CHINA GORMAN

Chair of WorkHuman Advisory Board for Globoforce;
former CEO of the Great Place to Work Institute

Developing a leadership-focused culture can create a cycle of success. Gorman believes an organization will attract talent by building a leadership-focused culture. "If you want the right employees, then you must tailor your culture to match what you are expecting in an employee," Gorman said. "A talented team will give its best work every day, no matter what." This mind-set leads to optimal results that typically exceed the expectations of all the stakeholders. "A fluid organization must have a general consensus on all levels, share more knowledge, and apply a greater level of transparency in order to build employee trust," she said.

Recruit to your culture. "Before recruiting talent, an organization must know what its culture is and what it is trying to achieve, so that its values are a palpable thing that everyone understands," Gorman said. "The organization's leaders must ask themselves: what values distinguish our organization from others? With this question in mind, those leaders can attract and recruit talent based on the organization's values."

Leaders must look for opportunities to build bonds of trust in their organization. "Faith and trust are integral to creating a value-based culture," Gorman said. "Trustworthy leaders have to be on good behavior day in and day out and must always seek opportunities to establish stronger bonds with their professional team. Whether they are making a statement or a decision, leaders must think conscientiously if their words will build trust within their culture or if those words will tear it down."

G. J. HART

CEO of California Pizza Kitchen

Trust is earned over time. "Trust is earned by the integrity expressed by employees to upper management and vice versa," Hart said. "This all develops from a process of assessing the business status of an organization, peeling back the layers, reviewing the resources and horsepower of the people, and understanding their immediate needs."

The creation of open communication forums breeds success. "I like to create platforms and places where people can get together and talk about issues and share best practices, all within an inviting environment," Hart said. "I desire for the people to have a voice and feel comfortable sharing their ideas. This helps everyone in the organization build upon each other in an encouraging way, celebrate success, and establish a stronger camaraderie, and it allows the upper management to get valuable time with their front-end employees."

SYLVIA HATCHELL

Head coach of University of North Carolina at Chapel Hill's women's basketball; AIAW, NAIA, and NCAA national champion

There's a difference between a good team and a good program. "A good program stands the test of time, through defeat, injury, and player turnover," Hatchell said. "Good programs embrace whatever changes arise and persevere through all challenges."

Appendix

TOM IZZO

Head coach of Michigan State University men's basketball,
(1995–present); 2000 national champion

Explain the "why." "I like to ensure that my players understand the reasoning behind my decisions, so I put an emphasis on explaining to my players why I coach the way I do," Izzo said.

Show interest in team members' personal goals. At the beginning of every season, Izzo has his players write five goals for the year on individual 3 x 5 note cards. His only instruction is for the players to be as "selfish" as possible. "I want to know my players' individual goals, not the goals for the team or what they think I want to hear," he said. "I then meet with every player individually to discuss those cards and to give each player my support or criticism in achieving those goals. My interest in my players' personal goals shows them that I care and makes them more receptive to tough criticism on the basketball court."

JIMMIE JOHNSON

Six-time NASCAR Sprint Cup Series champion

Keep a championship mentality. For Johnson and his team, sustained success comes from what he calls a "championship mentality." Johnson, his crew chief Chad Knaus, and his pit crew hold themselves to an incredibly high standard—which ultimately affects their level of preparation. "By having a championship mentality, my team and I feel a responsibility to continue performing at a high level," Johnson said.

Communication gives the edge. NASCAR regulations ensure that no driver can enhance his or her car to get an advantage over the competition. So what makes the difference between winners and losers, according to Johnson, is the human element. That's why "communication at all levels of the team is the key to success on the track."

216

MICHAEL JORDAN

Principal owner and chairman of the Charlotte Hornets;
six-time NBA champion for the Chicago Bulls

Find ways to put logs on your fire. Michael Jordan motivated himself by taking any possible slight from another player or the media—intentional or unintentional—personally. Even after he had become arguably the greatest player of all time, Jordan found ways to motivate himself by imagining that his opponents thought they could shut him down. "I am such a competitor that my opponents made me more competitive; they drove me to keep working and kept putting logs on my fire," Jordan said.

GREG KAMPE

Head coach of Oakland University men's basketball

Invest in recruiting to reduce turnover. "I look at the end of every year and watch literally hundreds of players transfer from one school to the other," Kampe said. "Some of those are because a coaching change occurred. Some are because of homesickness. But most of these kids transfer because they got to campus and realized they weren't at the right place. I believe that better recruiting—getting to know players and letting them get to know the real you—makes a huge difference in players staying, even when they aren't getting the playing time they hope for."

STEVE KERR

Head coach of the Golden State Warriors (2014–present); former point guard
for the Chicago Bulls and San Antonio Spurs; five-time NBA champion

Culture-building can turn a losing program around. "Culture building is the explanation for why losing organizations often become strong," Kerr said. "A Great Team develops foundations by knowing its strengths, recruiting great fits for the organization, and determining how the organization has to play."

Dynamic leadership spurs team effort. "The best coaches impose their will through charisma, principles, intelligence, and humor; they are 100 percent in charge, and their endearing qualities bring out the best in people," Kerr said. Kerr was exposed to this leadership in coaches Lute Olsen of the University of Arizona Wildcats, Phil Jackson of the Chicago Bulls, and Gregg Popovich of the San Antonio Spurs. He believes this kind of leadership helps get athletes to play really hard for each other.

Selfishness is innate, but it can be overcome. "We all want what's best for us, and in basketball this translates into shots-per-game, points, and notoriety," Kerr said. "But getting a group of high-performing people to sacrifice something for the team is the mark of a truly great organization. By defying our natural tendencies, we can become great."

MIKE KRZYZEWSKI
Head coach of Duke University men's basketball; five-time national champion; head coach of the USA men's national basketball team

Team culture is about the entire organization owning team values. "The values of an organization must permeate the entire team," Krzyzewski said. At Duke, values have an impact on everyone, all the way to the managers. When every member, no matter the role, knows the values of the team, the team culture will thrive.

Pay attention to body language. Krzyzewski critiques his players on their body language during practice. He shows players film of themselves on the sidelines or in a huddle and how their body language makes them appear disinterested. "Attentive body language sends a strong message of leadership, so I require my players to be attentive at all times," he said.

Make sure staff and managers are on board. At Duke,

Krzyzewski understands the importance of maintaining culture in the long term. He ensures that his office staff feels ownership of the program and that his managers understand they are as important to the team's success as the players they assist. "While players come and go, assistants, trainers, and office staff are with the program for longer periods of time," he said.

JENN LIM

CEO and CHO (Chief Happiness Officer) of
Delivering Happiness; motivational speaker

Find out who you are. Lim believes that every person in an organization needs to find out who he or she is. "The most important thing is to stay true to your authentic self—or your weird self—and put an emphasis on living out your passions, living out your sense of flow, and ultimately living out your purpose."

Find your purpose and align it with that of your company. "When I boil happiness down to its simplest form, I think that it's a sense of purpose." She believes employees should share the same values as their employers. "It is so important to align the individual's purpose with the company because even the person doing the most remedial job won't think of things as a task, but they will think of it as part of their career," she shared. "Anyone who walks through the door should think that they are the reason why the company exists."

Don't forget why you do what you do. "I worked with one company that knew culture and happiness was important to them, but they ended up growing so fast that they lost track of who they were in the process. They came to one of [my] speeches . . . but they couldn't really grasp what message I was trying to get across. Toward the end of our sessions, we had the CEO in tears because we made him realize [again] why he was doing what he was doing. . . . He had forgotten what it means for his company to have a sense of meaning and a sense of purpose."

ARCHIE MANNING

Former NFL quarterback (New Orleans Saints, Houston Oilers, and Minnesota Vikings); father of NFL quarterbacks Eli and Peyton Manning

Success comes from hard work. Manning impressed this upon sons Cooper, Peyton, and Eli at a young age. He told them, "The harder you work, the luckier you get."

It's important to let virtue be your guide. He raised his sons to be responsible and accountable and stressed leadership no matter what path they chose. "I tried to instill in them a moral compass," Manning said.

ELI MANNING

Quarterback for the New York Giants; two-time Super Bowl champion

Prepare well. "Daily practice is an opportunity to improve," Manning said.

Football and business are transferrable. "The success lessons in football are transferrable to any company," Manning said. "Commitment, hard work, and leadership can all carry over."

DAN MARINO

Former quarterback for the Miami Dolphins (1983–99)

Leadership comes naturally; it can't be forced. "Leadership comes by the example you set through your work," Marino said. "It begins from the way you are perceived as a worker and the respect that comes with it."

Don Shula was an influential leader. "Coach Shula was the best leader I ever met because of his even-keeled nature and tireless work ethic," Marino said.

Mental toughness helps you adapt. After his recovery from

an Achilles tendon injury, Marino had to adapt his game to fit his new physical limitations. "Mental toughness is an important part of adapting to new circumstances," he said.

MIKE MARTIN

Head coach of Florida State University baseball

Take responsibility for errors on the field. "The attitude of a leader bleeds down to his players," Martin said. "It's a coach's job to help players understand if errors are made on the field and to remain positive through adversity."

Everyone has value. Martin strives to make every player on his team understand his importance. This is especially true for the players at the end of his bench, the guys who aren't going to play anytime soon. These players have the potential to mentally check out from the culture of the team. Their attitudes can bring the whole team down. To combat this, Martin encourages his veterans to tell these young players they are needed. "Keeping players involved requires time and effort, but the best teams keep their organization engaged," he said.

Have a plan for the bottom ten. Martin also goes out of his way during the game to remind his bench players that he is looking out for them and wants to get them in the game when it is appropriate.

MISTY MAY-TREANOR

Three-time USA Olympic beach volleyball gold medalist

Work every advantage. When physical talent alone was not enough to dominate at the international level, May-Treanor and Kerri Walsh Jennings improved the mental side of their game and focused on improving their nutrition. "I recognized the skill and talent that got us to the top would not keep us there, so we planned accordingly,"

May-Treanor said. "We had to be willing to do and try different things to keep winning. I learned so much during that period about what it means and what it takes to be successful for the long haul . . . you have to be open to new approaches."

BILL MCDERMOTT

CEO of the multinational enterprise software company SAP SE

Great leaders have empathy. "Empathy is the greatest skill a leader needs to have," McDermott said. "A great leader can't go in with all the answers. The people have the answers. In a certain sense, when the people speak, the leader has to obey. And you obey by understanding the culture, understanding what the people need, and having the empathy to listen and design a vision and a strategy to fulfill those needs."

You must adapt in order to please the customer. "By getting involved, having empathy for the customers, caring about meeting their needs, and doing things for them that perhaps others didn't do before, you are going to be a winner," McDermott said.

Think outside of the box. By doing things that others would not have considered, such as starting an SAP job program for people with autism, McDermott and his company have strengthened their workforce with the unique set of skills their employees offer. SAP has a whole program that's built around training, recruiting, and of course, caring for individuals with different skill sets. "We value cultivating uniqueness," McDermott said.

DERIN MCMAINS

Director of mental conditioning, University of Notre Dame;
former sports psychologist for the San Francisco Giants (MLB)

Build it from the ground up. McMains trains minor-league players in mental toughness so that they'll be ready to contribute once they get to the major-league level. When clubs build up the team "at the foundational level," he said, "recruits are mentally prepared faster."

Self-talk matters. "The messages we receive and the messages we tell ourselves matter, and those messages can greatly affect an athlete's on-the-field performance," McMains said. "Positive self-talk is conducive to success. Players must create a narrative to build themselves up instead of breaking themselves down."

DAYTON MOORE

General manager of the Kansas City Royals

Build a culture that supports everyone. Moore believes that the front office exists to help the people on the field and to support the players, managers, coaches, training staff, and medical team do a better job.

Make recruiting decisions on the basis of character. "Character is the most important trait when considering anyone," Moore said. "The character test is one of the hardest things to predict and also the most crucial part of the analysis. If a player doesn't fit into your clubhouse or community, he will be a problem and eventually [his] poor choices are going to permeate and play out on the field. You have to have strong character to be able to manage through a lot of the crucial issues if you are going to be successful."

Create an organization that you want your family to be a part of. Moore believes an important question to ask yourself is, "Do you trust this individual to be around your family?" Players may be gifted in what they do, but if they can't apply those moral principles in their lives, then eventually their lives and careers will be a shipwreck.

JAMIE MOYER

Former MLB pitcher for Seattle Mariners, Philadelphia Phillies, and others; only pitcher in MLB to pitch a shutout in four consecutive decades

Scout your opponents. "My pitching notebooks included details not only on batters I had faced myself, but also on how those batters had fared against other pitchers on different teams," Moyer said. "I scouted possible opponents to get a sense of how to best approach the at-bat."

TOM OSBORNE

Former head coach of the University of Nebraska football team (three-time national champions); former congressman

Positive coaching works better than negative coaching. "Breaking down a player in order to build him back up is not as effective as positive reinforcement," Osborne said. "Great coaches teach their players, not humiliate or belittle them."

There are three ways to look at adversity. "One is to quit—which isn't productive—and another is to pass the blame on to someone else: a teammate, referee, or any other excuse," said Osborne. "Finally, adversity is an opportunity to learn about yourself. So after a loss, I encourage my players to look for takeaways on how to improve."

Give team members a way to tackle issues together. Osborne developed the idea of a Unity Council as a way to give his players a way to come together and address issues. Made up of two members from each position group, each Unity Council would meet with the strengthening coach. "The council has two roles: to address anything that the players felt interfered with team unity and to hand out punishment to players who broke team rules. The council has a disciplinary code, and we hand out points for infractions. The worse the infraction, the more points a player receives. The Unity Council gives players a voice in forming the culture of the team and places pressure on the players to ensure their teammates meet those standards."

CHUCK PAGANO

Head coach of the Indianapolis Colts

The only expectations that matter are internal expectations. When Pagano took over the Colts in 2012, expectations outside the program were low. "I told my players that the only expectations that mattered were their own and that we were going to set the bar high each Sunday," he said.

Go to what you trust. Pagano encourages his players to focus on the fundamentals of their jobs when things get hectic. "If every player focuses on his job and gives it 100 percent focus and effort, the outcome will work itself out," he said.

BOB REINHEIMER

Principal at Reinheimer & Co., LLC; former executive director at Duke Corporate Education

You get a culture either by default or by design. "A culture builds by default when, over time, colleagues associate more with one another and influence each other's worldview," Reinheimer said. "In this process, certain beliefs become commonly held. Cultures form spontaneously, and if they aren't shaped, they function ineffectively. Great leaders in an organizational setting, in a political setting, and certainly in an athletic setting don't leave that culture to chance. They don't want to get it by default; they want to get it by design."

Fundamental attitudes of leaders shape team culture. "Identity and relationship are organically a part of a Great Team's culture from the very beginning," Reinheimer said. "Companies determine their organizational structure based on how they view their employees. Open systems are welcoming to strangers and new recruits, while closed systems are more guarded, with stricter structuring."

Great Teams clarify values and beliefs, then communicate them broadly. "Teams who are great at culture building are clear on the beliefs that they want to instill," Reinheimer said. "They must determine what they think is important and why. Then they simply and authentically articulate what they believe and why they believe it. And they are consistent."

Culture attracts talent. "The right recruiting strategy brings in people who will, over time, strengthen and build the culture," Reinheimer said. "Bringing in the wrong player can cause a lot of damage and create a lot of friction."

JERRY RICE

Former San Francisco 49ers wide receiver (1985–2000);
three-time Super Bowl champion

Know your role on the field. Rice knew that his role on the 49ers' offense was to read the defense and run the correct route. "If I did my job to the best of my ability, I knew Montana or Young would get me the football," he said.

RUSS ROSE

Head coach of Penn State University women's
volleyball (seven-time national champions)

Great cultures embody principles. "Culture is established in every interaction," Rose said. "You have to search for opportunities with your players to embody or reinforce principles."

Don't live in the past. "I never wear a ring from a previous championship because once the banquet is over, I begin focusing on the next season," Rose said. His office doesn't contain any of his seven NCAA championship trophies either. And he even traded one of his championship rings to one of his kids for a marble.

DAVID ROSS

Catcher for the Chicago Cubs (2014–present); former catcher for
the Boston Red Sox, Atlanta Braves, and other MLB teams

Camaraderie begins from the top down. When he joined the Red Sox, Ross was surprised to see the ownership call a meeting of new players at the beginning of the season. "In this meeting, the ownership encouraged the players to bring up any advantages that were provided by their old teams so that Boston could replicate that," he said.

If you have a goal, talk about it. "I've never been around a team that talked about winning the World Series so much," Ross said. "Every day my teammates and I would . . . comment on how we were one day closer to winning the World Series."

Become the ultimate teammate. "I have been successful because of my willingness to assume whatever role the team needs and to deliver when asked," Ross said.

NOLAN RYAN

Houston Astros executive advisor; former CEO of Texas
Rangers; MLB Hall of Fame player for the New York Mets,
California Angels, Houston Astros, and Texas Rangers

Work hard every day. Nolan Ryan didn't just show up to work. He showed up *to work.* "I knew the importance of working hard and improving every day and wanted to prove that I belonged in the lineup," he said.

Diversify your training. Ryan's training coach would work with Japanese teams during the off-season and, when he returned, he'd walk Ryan through the strength and conditioning techniques he had observed overseas. Together, Ryan and his coach would incorporate the techniques into workouts.

Getting there is only half the battle. "To get to the professional ranks requires talent," Ryan said. "To remain in the professional ranks requires commitment and sacrifice."

Mental toughness and daily commitment are characteristics of greatness. At the beginning of his career, Ryan leaned on physical abilities too often. He would revert to throwing as hard and fast as possible when the going got tough. But over time he came to understand that he needed to develop other aspects of his game if he wanted to enjoy a long career. "I credit understanding the mental side of the sport and the importance of committing to daily improvement as keys to my longevity," he said.

SIMON SINEK

Author and motivational speaker

Determine your "why." "A 'why' is always disconnected from the product, service, or the act you're performing," Sinek said. "A 'why' for a sports team has nothing to do with their sport, and a 'why' for a company, if it's well formed, has nothing to do with the product. It's always about the immediate priority of the organization."

Order matters. "When an organization lays out its cause, the order matters," Sinek said. The "why" for many organizations is buried in context, but it has to come first in an organization. The order matters because it reveals whether you have a sense of purpose or not.

JERRY SLOAN

Former head coach of the Utah Jazz (1988–2011);
former NBA all-star for the Chicago Bulls

Top-level support is key. During Sloan's career with the Jazz, the team ownership never lost faith in him, even during tough stretches. The ownership's faith in Sloan to fix the problems allowed him to continue to keep his culture intact.

Have a game plan for the fourth quarter. "Teams rely on what they do well in the fourth quarter," Sloan said. For the Jazz, this meant running the pick-and-roll with John Stockton and Karl Malone.

There's no substitute for effort. Hard work was the founding principle of Sloan's culture with the Jazz. If a player wasn't giving 100 percent, Sloan would find someone else.

HENRY "TUBBY" SMITH

Head coach of University of Memphis men's basketball; former head coach at a
number of schools, including University of Kentucky; 1998 national champion

Be consistent. "Changing culture takes time," Smith said. "The keys are to be consistent in your approach and understand that longevity is the best tool to make a culture stick."

Embrace history and prepare for the future. "To embrace a culture, first, you have to understand the past, live in the present, and prepare for the future," Smith said. "Prepare your program, players, and yourself. You have to embrace history."

BILL SNYDER

Head coach of Kansas State University football (1989–2005, 2009–present)

Invest yourself. Coach Snyder does not take a job with the idea of being "half in." He approaches every coaching position with the mentality that it may be his last stop. This mentality allows him to set long-term goals for the program and build a solid foundation.

Character and talent go hand in hand. Coach Snyder looks for players who have character to go with their talent. "If you have good people, you have a chance," Snyder said.

Values should be seen as well as heard. "Priorities and values need to be defined," Snyder said. "Many people set goals, but very few accomplish them. One of the goals at Kansas State is to improve every day. So having physical reminders of a value or goal helps it become part of the culture."

BRENDAN SUHR

Associate coach of Louisiana State University men's basketball; former director of program development for University of Central Florida men's basketball; NBA assistant coach for nearly thirty years

Culture is created over time. "Culture is not an overnight development," Suhr said. "The staff, players, and coaches have to lead every day and be consistent in the culture-building process. A culture can easily develop negative characteristics, but keeping a cultural positive takes more effort."

Focus on five culture-based values. "An organization needs five values that tie in to their culture—no more, no less," Suhr said. "If those five values are important to you and your people, then they become what you live by."

The essentials in an organization are creativity, innovation, and character. "An organization needs people who are creative, innovative, and also have strong character," Suhr said. "Under pressure, people with character always rise to the occasion."

STAN VAN GUNDY

Head coach and president of basketball operations of the Detroit Pistons; former head coach of the Miami Heat and Orlando Magic

Creating a team culture is very important. Van Gundy believes it is a battle you need to fight every day by being on time, working hard, putting in extra work, and being a trustworthy teammate. "If a player shows poor effort or lack of preparation, then the team can correct those issues before they become a bad habit for everyone else," Van Gundy said.

No one is a jack-of-all-trades. "You cannot be good at everything," so "you must decide what you want to be good at," Van Gundy said. "You should focus on the four to five things that are important and those you can control, like hard work, putting the team first, toughness, and unselfishness. If a player does those things, then he won't have many problems."

Be "tough, smart, together." Van Gundy's developed his leaders with this philosophy. It meant being mentally tough as a team, making intelligent decisions, and having a collective direction.

BILL WALTON

NBA analyst; former player for the UCLA Bruins, Portland Trailblazers, Los Angeles Clippers, and Boston Celtics

Coach John Wooden taught life lessons. How do you react when the going gets tough? Walton points out that his UCLA coach John Wooden was consistent in his teaching and principles, even when the going got tough. Coach Wooden's teachings proved especially useful during difficult times in Walton's life. Whether it was a personal crisis or crunch time in a basketball game, the lessons and values from Wooden that he had blown off when things were going well always became important during the bad times.

Coach Wooden modeled selfless coaching. "Wooden was selfless, with no agendas and no level of self-promotion," Walton said. "He was a master at controlling his emotions and had no ego. He spent his life teaching and promoting the game of basketball, often giving free clinics and camps. Coach Wooden was a fundamentalist who specialized in defense, passing, and the fast break."

JERRY WEST

Former player, head coach, and general manager of the
Los Angeles Lakers; advisor to the Golden State Warriors

Look for a good fit. Jerry West believes that replacing departing leaders with leaders who fit the team's culture is vital to the survival of an organization. "It isn't enough to hire good employees; you need to hire good employees who fit the culture of the organization," he said.

Hire competent employees and trust their decisions. West believes employees are the foundation of a franchise and that ownership must trust the opinions of key personnel. He cites the decision to release Monta Ellis from Golden State as an example. The owner trusted that West was making the right decision.

The team is greater than the self. "A Great Team has integrity, experience, and is unafraid of criticism," West said. "Most importantly, the team members realize that the sum is greater than the individual."

Depth is crucially important. He equates not having a capable replacement to missing a piece in the middle of your puzzle. Additionally, a good coach has a plan to replace key players. Players who are willing to accept a bench role are invaluable to the team.

JOHN WOODEN

Former head coach of UCLA men's basketball
(1948–75); ten-time NCAA champion

Start on time and end on time. Wooden never let practice run late. He believed players would give more effort if they knew how long they had left.

Never lose your composure. Wooden taught that when things don't go as planned, a leader needs to maintain an appearance of calm.

A great leader is a great teacher. Wooden had a philosophy that a leader should strive to teach his players how to improve, how to win, and how to be a teammate.

Leadership involves selling your vision. Wooden believed that a great leader knows how to sell the team on the way he or she sees the organization.

A leader needs to innovate. Wooden's first championship squad didn't have a player over six-foot-five, so he recruited for his needs and signed Kareem Abdul-Jabbar the next year for his UCLA Bruins. Wooden's Bruins demonstrated adaptability in that both teams won championships with different strategies.

Do the little things right. Wooden approached every part of his teaching from the fundamental level. The first practice of every season for Wooden's Bruins was a lesson in how to properly put on shoes and socks. As he loved to say, "If you don't have time to do it right, when will you have time to do it over?"

Never stop learning. After every season Wooden would sit down with his assistant coaches and determine one aspect of their team that could be improved. Once staff figured out what they needed to improve, they would pinpoint a college team that did something better than UCLA. Wooden would then handwrite a letter to the coach of that team, asking if he could visit to learn from him firsthand.

STEVE YOUNG

Former San Francisco 49ers quarterback (1987–99);
three-time Super Bowl champion

Competition makes you better, even on your own team. While backing up Joe Montana, Young was constantly pushing Montana for playing time. "This competition made both of us better," Young said.

Know your role in the huddle. Young's role was to communicate the play call to his teammates. Under Bill Walsh, the quarterback was the only player allowed to talk in the huddle.

ACKNOWLEDGMENTS

N o book like this becomes real without a Great Team surrounding the author. This project was made possible only because my team made it so.

The great organizational and writing talent of Lee Williams kept this book on track from the day the concept was sold. Tiffany Brooks, who has been my partner on a dozen book projects over the last decade, was a gift as an in-house editor. I owe you both. Elton Gumbel from my speaking team has artfully built this into a keynote presentation and ongoing Great Teams web series that allows me to share these stories with companies around the globe. Anjie Cheatham, who manages the speaking piece of my life, has made it her goal that I get to share my Great Teams speech often because she so believes in the subject.

There would have been nothing to write or speak about, though, if the more than one hundred team builders, coaches, and thought leaders who participated here hadn't agreed to give their time and their energy to this discussion. I will always be grateful for the education each of you provided, and I hope I treated your thoughts respectfully.

In my opinion this project went from good to great when Dr. Leff Bonney from the Florida State University College of Business built business lessons around the habits I was learning from these great culture builders. Dr. Bonney's passion for athletics made him the perfect partner, providing the meat to the bones of my stories.

My agent, Ian Kleinert from Objective Entertainment, was an early believer that this project could be a winner, and we were blessed that Matt Baugher, Senior Vice President and Publisher of W Publishing Group, agreed. Matt lined me up with the best editors imaginable in Meaghan

Acknowledgments

Porter and Joel Kneedler. W Publishing then handed me over to the amazing publicity team led by Lori Cloud. Without each of you, this doesn't come close to its potential.

Two powerful influences both on this book and on my passion for studying excellence were two of the finest college basketball coaches (and extraordinary men) I've been able to call friends: LSU's Dale Brown and UCLA's John Wooden. My world is better because they have been in it.

One of America's great sportswriters, Jason Cole, was a wonderful resource. He had so many stories to offer and adding them to my learning made this book more complete.

Like Coaches Brown and Wooden, several world-class business executives have helped me grow and are a significant piece of this book: Microsoft's Eric Martorano (mentioned in the introduction for encouraging me to begin this study), Oracle's Bill Swales, Brocade's Anthony Robbins, Visalus founder Ryan Blair, and Col. Bernard Banks became, collectively, the "kitchen cabinet" that discussed and challenged me with these subjects regularly.

On the personal side, my wife, Jeanette, has been the partner I've always dreamed of. She—and our children, Will and Maddie—made it tough to travel for all these interviews because home is absolutely where my heart is.

NOTES

INTRODUCTION: WHAT MAKES A TEAM GREAT?

1. Don Yaeger, *Greatness: The 16 Characteristics of True Champions* (New York: Center Street, 2011).
2. Unless otherwise noted, all quotations are from interviews with the author.

CHAPTER 1: GREAT TEAMS UNDERSTAND THEIR "WHY"

1. "The Declaration of Independence: A Transcription," July 4, 1776, in The Charters of Freedom, United States National Archives online exhibit, http://www.archives.gov/exhibits/charters/declaration_transcript.html.
2. Susan Sorenson and Keri Garman, "How to Tackle U. S. Employees' Stagnating Engagement," *Business Journal,* June 11, 2013, Gallup.com, http://www.gallup.com/businessjournal/162953/tackle-employees -stagnating-engagement.aspx.

CHAPTER 2: GREAT TEAMS HAVE AND DEVELOP GREAT LEADERS

1. John Wooden and Jay Carty, *Coach Wooden's Pyramid of Success* (Ventura, CA: Regal Books, 2009), 17.
2. G. Andrew Boyd, "John Wooden Retrospective: Bill Walton on How John Wooden Changed His Life," *Times-Picayune* (New Orleans), April 2, 1993, http://www.nola.com/sports/index.ssf/2010/06/john_wooden _retrospective_bill.html.
3. Jerry Hirsch, "Wooden's Tips for Courting Success," *Los Angeles Times,* June 2, 2008, http://articles.latimes.com/2008/jun/02/business /fi-wooden2.
4. ESPN.com staff, "The Wizard's Wisdom: 'Woodenisms,'" ESPN.com, June 5, 2010, http://espn.go.com/ncb/news/story?id=5249709.
5. Ibid.

6. Ibid.

7. Sven Nater and Ronald Gallimore, *You Haven't Taught Until They Have Learned: John Wooden's Teaching Principles and Practices* (Morgantown, WV: Fitness Information Technology, 2006), 103.

CHAPTER 3: GREAT TEAMS ALLOW CULTURE TO SHAPE RECRUITING

1. Kevin Ryan, "Gilt Groupe's CEO on Building a Team of A Players," *Harvard Business Review*, January–February 2012, https://hbr.org/2012 /01/gilt-groupes-ceo-on-building-a-team-of-a-players.

2. Steve Greenberg, "College Football Coach Rankings: Nos. 1–124," *Sporting News*, May 9, 2012, http://www.sportingnews.com/list/2794292 -college-football-coach-rankings-nick-saban-chris-petersen-urban-meyer -les-miles/slide/93484.

3. Michael C. Mankins, Alan Bird, and James Root, "Making Star Teams Out of Star Players, *Harvard Business Review,* January–February 2013, https://hbr.org/2013/01/making-star-teams-out-of-star-players/ar/.

4. Tony Hsieh, "How Zappos Infuses Culture Using Core Values," *Harvard Business Review*, May 24, 2010, https://hbr.org/2010/05/how-zappos -infuses-culture-using-core-values.

5. "Corporate Overview," Target.com, http://investors.target.com/phoenix .zhtml?c=65828&p=irol-homeProfile&_ga=1.25323449.528101078.14 59174395; "Purpose and Beliefs," Target.com, https://corporate.target .com/about/purpose-beliefs; "Spotlight on Target's Hispanic Business Council," Target.com, July 23, 2013, https://corporate.target.com/article /2013/07/spotlight-on-target-s-hispanic-business-council.

6. United States Census Bureau, "Millennials Outnumber Baby Boomers and Are Far More Diverse, Census Bureau Reports," news release, June 25, 2015, https://www.census.gov/newsroom/press-releases/2015/cb15-113 .html.

7. Rob Asghar, "What Millennials Want in the Workplace (And Why You Should Start Giving It to Them)," *Forbes,* January 13, 2014, http://www .forbes.com/sites/robasghar/2014/01/13/what-millennials-want-in-the -workplace-and-why-you-should-start-giving-it-to-them/#50e280432fdf.

8. Stephen R. Covey, *The 8th Habit: From Effectiveness to Greatness* (New York: Free Press, 2004), 77.

CHAPTER 4: GREAT TEAMS CREATE AND MAINTAIN DEPTH

1. Larry Reynolds, "Retaining Workers in 2014 Requires Clear Talent-Retention Strategy, Counteroffer Guide," *Bulletin to Management,* January 8, 2014, posted on Bloomberg BNA website, http://www.bna.com /retaining-workers-2014-n17179881224/.

2. Anne Fisher, "Telltale Signs Your Star Employees Are Job Hunting," *Fortune,* August 16, 2013, http://fortune.com/2013/08/16/telltale-signs -your-star-employees-are-job-hunting/?iid=sr-link5.

CHAPTER 5: GREAT TEAMS HAVE A ROAD MAP

1. Jim McElwain, interviewed on *The Herd, with Colin Cowherd*, ESPN Radio, September 18, 2013, available as podcast on ESPN website at http:// espn.go.com/espnradio/play?id=9689181.

2. John Wooden and Jay Carty, *Coach Wooden's Pyramid of Success* (Ventura, CA: Regal Books, 2009), 26–27.

3. Many versions of this list have circulated. This one is taken from Mark Janssen, "SE: K-States '16 Goals' Go Back to Snyder's Youth," *K-State Sports Extra* (e-mail newsletter), reproduced on K-State Athletics website, http://www.kstatesports.com/news/sports_m-footbl_spec-rel_122112 aaa_html.

4. "The Nestlé Roadmap to Good Food, Good Life," *Nestlé Annual Report 2012*, 18. PDF document accessed at http://docslide.us/documents/2012 -annual-report-enpdf.html. A visual representation of the road map can be found at http://www.nestle.com/aboutus/strategy.

5. Ibid., 16.

6. Ibid., 18.

7. Ibid.

8. Ibid.

9. "Constantly Challenge Your Vision," interview with Cheryl Bachelder, video transcript, Leadercast Now, n.d., accessed March 1, 2016, https:// www.leadercast.com/now/leadership-principles/constantly-challenge -your-vision/.

10. Adam Lashinsky, "Facebook's Earnings: Internet Do-gooderism and Ad Gobbledygook," *Fortune,* January 28, 2015, http://fortune.com/2015 /01/28/facebook-do-gooderism-gobbledygook/.

11. Alyson Shontell, "Mark Zuckerberg Just Revealed His Grand Vision for

the Next 10 Years of Facebook," *Business Insider,* October 29, 2014, http://
www.businessinsider.com/zuckerbergs-3–5-and-10-year-facebook-plan
-2014–10.

12. Mark Zuckerberg, "Mark Zuckerberg Live Video at Facebook HQ
(Introducing New Facebook Office Inside)," YouTube video, 3:15,
September 15, 2015, https://www.youtube.com/watch?v=l—zev_37QA.

CHAPTER 6: GREAT TEAMS PROMOTE CAMARADERIE AND A SENSE OF COLLECTIVE DIRECTION

1. Mike Monroe, "Pop Pays Homage to Patty Mills' Culture, Family," *San Antonio Express-News,* June 6, 2014, http://www.expressnews.com/sports
/spurs/article/Pop-pays-homage-to-Patty-Mills-culture-family-5535351.php.

2. Don Yaeger, "Vision, Value, and Voice: The Real Magnet of Team Success,"
Forbes, July 28, 2015, http://www.forbes.com/sites/donyaeger/2015/07/28
/vision-value-and-voice-the-real-magnet-of-team-success/#1010675a2ca4.

3. David Muir, "Meet Nick, a Hugger and Healer," video segment originally
aired on *ABC World News Tonight,* 2:52, April 24, 2014, posted on ABC
News website, accessed March 5, 2016, http://abcnews.go.com/WNT/
video/meet-nick-hugger-healer-23462925.

4. Yaeger, "Vision, Value, and Voice."

5. Ibid.

CHAPTER 7: GREAT TEAMS MANAGE DYSFUNCTION, FRICTION, AND STRONG PERSONALITIES

1. Roy Taylor, "Ditka vs. Ryan: Grudgematches 1986–1989," Chicago Bears
History website, http://bearshistory1.brinkster.net/lore/ditkaandryan
.aspx.

2. *Workplace Conflict and How Businesses Can Harness It to Thrive,* CPP
Global Human Capital Report, June 2008, cited in Jennifer Lawler, "The
Real Cost of Workplace Conflict," Entrepreneur.com, June 21, 2010,
http://www.entrepreneur.com/article/207196.

3. Kenneth W. Thomas and Ralph H. Kilmann, "An Overview of the
Thomas-Kilmann Conflict Mode Instrument (TKI)," Kilmann
Diagnostics website, http://www.kilmanndiagnostics.com/overview
-thomas-kilmann-conflict-mode-instrument-tki.

4. Information in this section based on Jeff Weiss and Jonathan Hughes,
"Want Collaboration? Accept—and Actively Manage—Conflict," in Joan

V. Gallos, ed., *Business Leadership: A Jossey-Bass Reader* (San Francisco: Jossey-Bass, 2008), 359–361; previously published in *Harvard Business Review* 83, no. 3 (2005); 92–101.

CHAPTER 8: GREAT TEAMS BUILD A MENTORING CULTURE

1. Octagon Speakers Group, "Bob Bowman, Swimming Coach of Michael Phelps—An Introduction," YouTube video, 5:07, March 30, 2010, https://www.youtube.com/watch?v=PJrar4Wym1w.
2. Childs Walker, "Bob Bowman Named Head Coach for 2016 U.S. Olympic Swimming Team," *Baltimore Sun,* September 9, 2015, http://www.baltimoresun.com/sports/olympics/olympics/bs-sp-bob-bowman-olympic-coach-20150909-story.html.
3. Childs Walker, "Bob Bowman's Move to Arizona Comes as 'Post-Michael' Phelps Era Nears," *Baltimore Sun,* May 31, 2015, http://www.baltimoresun.com/sports/olympics/bs-sp-bob-bowman-0601-20150531-story.html.
4. J. A. Adande, "Spurs Admiration Starts with Admiral," ESPN.com, May 30, 2012, http://espn.go.com/nba/playoffs/2012/story/_/id/7982610/nba-playoffs-san-antonio-spurs-success-traces-back-david-robinson.
5. Scott Pioli, quoted in Christopher Price, *The Blueprint: How the New England Patriots Beat the System to Create the Last Great NFL Superpower* (New York: Thomas Dunne Books, 2007), 302.
6. Sean Bryant, "The Best Fortune 500 Mentorship Programs (GE, INTC)," February 23, 2015, http://www.investopedia.com/articles/personal-finance/022315/best-fortune-500-mentorship-programs.asp.
7. Zana Zidansek, "Top Development Programs in Industrial Products & Service Industry," MBA-Exchange.com, http://www.mba-exchange.com/candidates/Top-Development-Programs-in-Industrial-Products-and-Services-Industry-690-session-.
8. "Experienced Program: Experienced Commercial Leadership Program (ECLP), Global," GE (website), http://www.ge.com/careers/culture/university-students/experienced-commercial-leadership-program/global.
9. Fara Warner, "Inside Intel's Mentoring Movement," *Fast Company,* March 31, 2002, http://www.fastcompany.com/44814/inside-intels-mentoring-movement.

CHAPTER 9: GREAT TEAMS ADJUST QUICKLY TO LEADERSHIP TRANSITIONS

1. Adam Fluck, "Pippen Stood Tall Without Jordan in 1993–94," NBA. com, May 20, 2014, http://www.nba.com/bulls/history/pippen-stood-tall -without-jordan-1993–94.
2. Adam Fluck, "Jackson: Pippen an Obvious Choice for Hall of Fame," NBA.com, July 28, 2010, http://www.nba.com/bulls/history/pippenhof _jackson_100730.html.
3. Tony Manfred, "Here's the Perfect 2-Word Statement Michael Jordan Sent Out to Announce His Return to the NBA 20 Years Ago," *Business Insider,* March 18, 2015, http://www.businessinsider.com /michael-jordan-im-back-fax-2015–3.
4. Melissa Isaacson, "More Than a Sidekick, Pippen a Partner," *Chicago Tribune,* January 24, 1999, http://articles.chicagotribune.com/1999–01–24 /sports/9901240037_1_scottie-pippen-pippen-and-grant-bulls.
5. Ibid.
6. Sharon Price John, "Meet the Woman Who Rescued Build-A-Bear Workshop," *Fortune,* July 14, 2015, http://fortune.com/2015/07/14/sharon -price-john-dealing-with-change/.
7. Ibid.

CHAPTER 10: GREAT TEAMS ADAPT AND EMBRACE CHANGE

1. Although this quotation—and many variations of it—is usually attributed to Darwin, it cannot be found in any of his written work. The probable source for the quote is a much less succinct version in a 1963 speech by LSU business professor Leon C. Megginson. For more information see Garson O'Toole, "It Is Not the Strongest of the Species That Survives but the Most Adaptable," *Quote Investigator: Exploring the Origins of Quotations,* http://quoteinvestigator.com/tag/leon-c-megginson/.
2. Sami Lais, "Verizon: Not Just a Phone Company," *Washington Technology,* May 7, 2009, https://washingtontechnology.com/Articles/2009/05/11/Top -100-Verizon-16.aspx.
3. Ibid.
4. Ibid.
5. Jeremy Weisz, "Girl Scouts of America: Presidential Medal of Freedom & Top Leadership—with Frances Hesselbein," InspiredInsider.com, accessed

March 2, 2016, http://www.inspiredinsider.com/frances-hesselbein-girl
scoutsofamerica-interview/.

CHAPTER 11: GREAT TEAMS RUN SUCCESSFUL HUDDLES

1. Sue Shellenbarger, "Don't Be the Office Schedule-Wrecker," *Wall Street Journal,* July 7, 2015, http://www.wsj.com/articles/dont-be-the-office
-schedule-wrecker-1436290208.
2. Adam Lashinsky, "How Apple Works: Inside the World's Biggest Startup," *Fortune,* May 9, 2011, http://fortune.com/2011/05/09/inside-apple/.
3. Kristen Gil, "Start-Up Speed," *Think with Google,* January 2012, https://www.thinkwithgoogle.com/articles/start-up-speed-kristen-gil.html.
4. Ibid.
5. Ibid.

CHAPTER 12: GREAT TEAMS IMPROVE THROUGH SCOUTING

1. Mike Gastineau, "A Glorious Moment Recalled: 1980 'Miracle on Ice,'" SportspressNW.com, http://sportspressnw.com/2179612/2014/a-glorious
-moment-recalled-1980-miracle-on-ice.
2. Cover photograph by Heinz Kleutmeier, *Sports Illustrated* 52 no. 9 (March 3, 1980), http://www.si.com/vault/issue/70874/1/1?cover_view=1.
3. J. Kroon, *General Management,* 2nd ed. (Pretoria: Kasigo Tertiary, 1995), 76.
4. Robert Trigaux, "Publix Retains Iron Grip on No. 1 Spot in Florida's Competitive Grocery Business," *Tampa Bay Times,* November 3, 2015, http://www.tampabay.com/news/business/retail/publix-retains-iron-grip
-at-no1601-spot-in-floridas-competitive-grocery/2252386.
5. Susanna Kim, "Six Reasons Why Grocery Customers Love Publix," ABC News website, October 31, 2014, http://abcnews.go.com/Business
/reasons-grocery-customers-love-publix/story?id=26580508.
6. Ovidijus Jurevicius, "SWOT Analysis—Do It Properly!" Strategic Management Insight, February 13, 2013, https://www.strategic
managementinsight.com/tools/swot-analysis-how-to-do-it.html.
7. Spencer Soper, "Amazon CEO Jeff Bezos Promises Wall Street a Profit, *Bloomberg Business,* October 22, 2015, http://www.bloomberg.com/news
/articles/2015–10–23/amazon-ceo-jeff-bezos-promises-wall-street-a-profit
8. Ibid.

9. Nameer, "The Evolution of Benchmarking: The Xerox Case," *Total Quality Management* (blog), September 16, 2009, https://totalquality management.wordpress.com/2009/09/16/the-evolution-of-benchmarking -xerox-case/#more-1076.

CHAPTER 13: GREAT TEAMS SEE VALUE OTHERS MISS

1. Grantland Features, *The Coach Who Never Punts*, video short, dir. Jon Frankel, November 13, 2013, http://grantland.com/features/grantland- channel-coach-never-punts/, viewed March 3, 2016 on Vimeo, https:// vimeo.com/98478663. See also Adam Himmelsbach, "Punting Less Can Be Rewarding, but Coaches Aren't Risking Jobs on It," *New York Times,* August 18, 2012, http://www.nytimes.com/2012/08/19/sports/football /calculating-footballs-risk-of-not-punting-on-fourth-down.html.
2. "Football State Championships," Pulaski Academy Bruin Athletics, accessed March 2, 2016, http://www.pulaskiacademy.org/Page/Compete /Sports/Football#.
3. Michael Lewis, *Moneyball: The Art of Winning an Unfair Game* (New York: W. W. Norton, 2003). The 2011 film version of *Moneyball* was adapted for screen by Stan Chervin, Steve Zaillian, and Aaron Sorkin; directed by Bennett Miller; and released on DVD in 2012 by Sony Home Entertainment.

CHAPTER 14: GREAT TEAMS WIN IN CRITICAL SITUATIONS

1. Holland Reynolds, quoted in Kory Kozak, *The Finish Line: The Full Story*, ESPN, short film, https://www.youtube.com/watch?v=OrTtDxd-4iY.
2. "Analysis: Case Study—The Johnson & Johnson Tylenol Crisis," Crisis Communication Strategies, Department of Defense Joint Course in Communication, Class 02-C, Team 1, posted on University of Oklahoma website, www.ou.edu/deptcomm/dodjcc/groups/02C2/Johnson & Johnson.htm.
3. Tom W. Smith, Peter Marsden, Michael Hout, and Jibum Kim, General Social Surveys, 1972–2014. The GSS is a project of the independent research organization NORC at the University of Chicago, with principal funding from the National Science Foundation.
4. Florida State University Sales Institute, Sales Force Effectiveness Benchmarking Study, 2015.

5. Derek Dean and Caroline Webb, "Recovering from Information Overload," *McKinsey Quarterly*, January 2011, http://www.mckinsey .com/business-functions/organization/our-insights/recovering-from -information-overload.

CHAPTER 15: GREAT TEAMS SPEAK A DIFFERENT LANGUAGE

1. Dwyane Wade, "15 Strong: It's More Than a Slogan, It's a Burning Desire," forward to John Hareas and John Fawaz, *15 Strong: 2006 NBA Champion Miami Heat: The Official NBA Finals 2006 Retrospective*, NBA.com, http://www.nba.com/features/15strong_060713.html.
2. Bruce Jones, "3 Lessons in Creating a Magical Service Experience," *Talking Point* (blog), May 30, 2013, https://disneyinstitute.com/ blog/2013/05/3-lessons-in-creating-a-magical-customer-experience/168/.
3. Dennis Snow, "Employee Recognition—The Guest Service Fanatic," YouTube video, 2:55, August 29, 2010, https://www.youtube.com/watch ?v=A-ZlYBps1p0.
4. Jeff James, "Encouraging and Motivating Leaders," *Talking Point* (blog), April 19, 2012, https://disneyinstitute.com/blog/2012/04/encouraging-and -motivating-leaders/52/.
5. Adi Ignatius, "The HBR Interview: 'We Had to Own the Mistakes,'" *Harvard Business Review* 88, no. 7 (2010), https://hbr.org/2010/07/the-hbr -interview-we-had-to-own-the-mistakes.
6. Ibid.

CHAPTER 16: GREAT TEAMS AVOID THE PITFALLS OF SUCCESS

1. "The Wizard's Wisdom: 'Woodenisms,'" ESPN.com, June 5, 2010, http:// espn.go.com/mens-college-basketball/news/story?id=5249709.
2. Paul Meehan, Darrell Rigby, and Paul Rogers, "Creating and Sustaining a Winning Culture," *Harvard Business Review* 86, no. 1 (2008), originally published in *Harvard Management Update*, January 2008, https://hbr.org/ 2008/02/creating-and-sustaining-a-winn-1.
3. Glenn Llopis, "The Most Successful Companies Embrace the Promise of their Culture," *Forbes*, September 12, 2011, http://www.forbes.com/sites /glennllopis/2011/09/12/the-most-successful-companies-embrace-the -promise-of-their-culture/#41d20ec677bb.

Notes

4. Emmie Martin, "A Major Airline Says There's Something It Values More Than Its Customers, and There's a Good Reason Why," *Business Insider,* July 29, 2015, http://www.businessinsider.com/southwest-airlines -puts-employees-first-2015-7.

5. Ibid.

6. "Southwest Airlines 'Gets It' with Our Culture," *Nuts about Southwest* (blog), March 22, 2011, http://www.blogsouthwest.com/southwest-airlines -%E2%80%9Cgets-it%E2%80%9D-our-culture/.

ABOUT THE AUTHOR

As the author of more than two dozen books, nine of which have become *New York Times* bestsellers, **Don Yaeger** has developed a reputation as one of America's most provocative journalists. His award-winning writing career, including more than ten years as associate editor of *Sports Illustrated*, has led to guest appearances on every major talk show in America—from *Oprah* to *Nightline*, from *Fox News* to *Good Morning America*.

Today, Yaeger spends much of his time sharing lessons he's learned throughout his career with audiences across the country as an in-demand keynote speaker. He also does monthly virtual presentations on greatness with companies. His two primary presentations focus on the habits of individual high performers and, as with this book, the lessons businesses can learn from Great Teams.

He lives in Tallahassee, Florida, with his wife, Jeanette, and their son, Will, and daughter, Madeleine.

To learn more about Don, visit **www.donyaeger.com**.

CONTINUING YOUR
PURSUIT

Identifying your leadership style is a great first step. *But what kind of leadership style does your team need from you?*

BUILDING CHAMPIONSHIP CULTURES

WHAT MAKES THE
GREAT TEAMS GREAT

16 BUSINESS LESSONS LEARNED FROM ALL-TIME GREAT TEAMS

WORKBOOK

LESSON 1

As a bonus for purchasing this book, additional exercises on how your leadership style fits with your team are available!

FREE DOWNLOAD AT
teams.donyaeger.com

Grit & Glue

Take your FREE survey at

TEAMS.DONYAEGER.COM

Great Teams consistently demonstrate behaviors and chemistry that others don't.

From our qualitative and quantitative research, which includes years of measuring thousands of teams and discovering what makes the Great stand out, we consistently see differences in the depth of their relationship and engagement. They have an unusual level of what we describe as Grit & Glue.

Grit

They have a drive to work harder, make greater commitments, have a deeper purpose, demonstrate the fortitude needed to advance in the face of adversity, and a stronger resilience with the ability to adapt and bounce back.

Glue

They have a greater commitment to one another's success, greater team character, stronger unity and shared responsibility, an 'other' focus, strong chemistry and teamability, with better communication and deeper trust.

A Great Team's Grit & Glue is developed by talent, a desire to achieve what others have not, consistent effort, effective leadership, and a strong commitment to a disciplined process.

+ As a **FREE** feature of this book, you will have the benefit of measuring your team's **Grit & Glue!**

 IN PARTNERSHIP WITH